I0074541

Mind the Dy

The Garden Effect Model

Antonis Gavalas, MSc

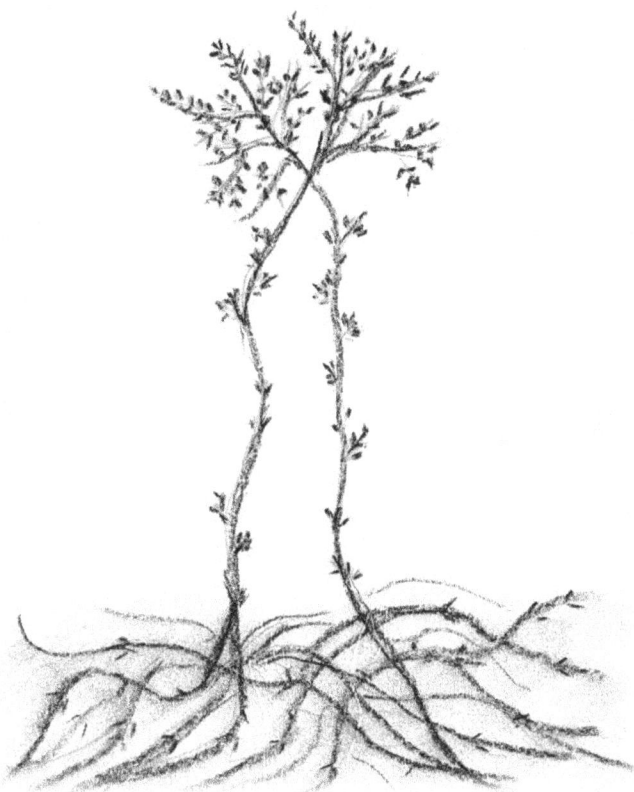

Equilibrium Management Systems

Title: *Mind the Dynamics: The Garden Effect Model*
Author: *Antonis Gavalas, MSc*
Category: *Equilibrium Management Systems*

Proofreading: Maria Tombazou – mariatomb@yahoo.com
Cover picture: Maria Gavala
Cover design: Dimitris Kouroukidis – dkouroukidis@gmail.com

First published in Greece by Antonis Gavalas, January 2016

ISBN: 978-618-80420-4-9

© 2016, by Antonis Gavalas

All rights reserved. No portion of this book may be reproduced, stored in an electronic retrieval system or transmitted in any form or by any means – electronic, mechanical, photocopy, recording, or any other – in English or in any other language without the prior permission of the author.

Published by:
Antonis Gavalas
T: +30 693 61 73 103
E: gavalasresearch@yahoo.com
www.antonisgavalas.com

Contents

Abbreviations

GEM: Garden Effect Model

KSAOs: Knowledge, Skills, Abilities, and other Personal Characteristics

KPI: Key Performance Index

RCT: Roles – Communication – Trust

To a world of freed mind and logic,
for my family to grow up in

Prologos

Through the years of my experience I came to the conclusion that business or team management is a trifold dynamic function consisted of three distinct but interdepended factors: People, Processes, and Resources. Take one of these dimensions out of the equation and the balance will be disturbed with deteriorating effects for your organization's performance. The current book is a practical guide of a dynamic management model, which will help you build a successful team or organization, based on **an equilibrium system which brings balance between diverse forces** such as knowledge, skills, personalities, feelings, and personal ambitions.

Knowledge cannot all be included in 100 pages nor in 10,000 pages. There are many theories and techniques which could fit you. The goal of reading this book is more about understanding the concept behind the suggested model. Use the tools and the tips provided wisely. Remember that you are not alone; you have your people around you. **Use your strengths to compensate for each other's weaknesses.**

In practice, the pillars of this management approach are the roles (which include resources as well) and the interpersonal relationships. These two dimensions include all the factors affecting how things work between people, such as role positions and personal characteristics. You need to implement this model as a team, to open up one another honestly and supportively.

Think of people and roles as a system of interacting factors. You cannot separate any of them because then the system will collapse. You may design the best processes and use the most sophisticated technology, but if your people are far away from performing there is no point in having any of these. Or you may have the most capable and talented people under your supervision but if roles are unclear and processes are a mess, they will never perform as much as they can, their talents will never be shown.

Thinking of leadership, there is an extended literature analyzing the type and the effective leader. It is mostly based on behavioral change and personal awareness. They all are sound theories accounting for much of the leadership success. However, one becomes a leader by practicing leadership, and there is no better way to do that than by creating the right context that will give you the opportunity to exert the best leadership behaviors (Kouzes & Posner, 2003). Don't forget that you are just another role in the system, just another person interacting with other people. Your role also creates and affects the dynamics in total.

Follow the dynamic system approach provided here and you will be able to become a better leader, in practice and not in theory. Your people will feel your support, your understanding, your caring, and your effort to help them become better persons personally and professionally. They will reciprocate the support, once you are a part of the process. Participate in the model's implementation, include your role into the process, know yourself and your people, and most importantly become explicitly committed to its success. As a leader, you need not to be over their shoulders looking at every step they make nor to be giving every small detailed order. Once you have set the context and have given the right directions, you can leave the system grow itself. **They know the way.**

The Model

This model is a tool developed based on organizational behavior, management, psychology and neuroscience research. These disciplines have offered us great insights on **how people act, react, and interact**. The main dimension of this model's approach is that people need to be free to think and fulfil their own ambitions. Personal engagement is translated into motivation, an emotional attachment which activates the appropriate brain fields which in turn increase focus, and memory (Kandel et al, 2011). Positive reward and supportive leadership **foster mind engagement and not "encagement"**.

Create an open, trustful, and fearless environment. People do not react well to fear, they entrench themselves or they run away (Kliegel & Jager, 2006). They do not openly communicate and they do not aim their energy and effort, nor their focus, toward the right direction. Increased attention is what provides people with the right amounts of energy to learn new things, and readily accept change. I suggest **a threefold leadership goal**: *set the context, let your people free to act, be there for them when they lose focus*. Just as simple as that.

I hereunder present an outline of the dynamic management system that will allow you to set the context in order to leave your people free to act within an ever-learning environment. For that you need a clear view of the organizational future, clear and understandable roles. You also need to know your people in order to bring the best out of them, and help them interact and cooperate effectively.

Dynamics are mainly determined by:

- Roles (including resources and other working environmental factors)
- Personal characteristics

These two main dimensions are further analyzed into formal and informal factors. Formal factors are those mainly determined by role descriptions and relationships affected by role and core personal characteristics. Informal factors are those determined by personal interactions, likeness, and the role of emotions in relationships and performance. More specifically:

Formal factors are:

- Role details
- Position's power
- Interpersonal relationships

Informal factors are:

- Sympathy
- Emotions

Up till here we have specified the core dimensions of a dynamic model. However, in order to deploy this model you will need some enablers who will support the success of this system.

Enablers

- Leadership
- Trust
- Communication
- Development opportunities

First and foremost is leadership, which is another role within the system, but since leaders have the responsibility of their people, it is most important to support the delivery of a successful management system (**leadership in practice**). Leaders are those fostering the cultural integration of a high performing approach. For that they need to build the other important enablers, which are trust, communication, and the opportunities that their people will be provided with for personal and professional growth (motivation).

Culture

Culture is the environmental factor that includes and fosters everything else. Embedding the dynamic management approach into your culture will elevate your leadership maturity level. Some cultural dimensions presented here, important for high performing organizations, refer to synergy development, supportiveness and cover up behaviors, as well as how you should develop a learning organization.

High Performing Organization

Speaking of high performing organizations or teams I also present the trifold *Roles – Communication – Trust* (the upside down triangle) approach as the least required index for building the foundations of performance. Score highly on that index and you will have a well-functioning and highly performing organization, capable to build through motivation on even higher engagement, commitment and of course corporate achievements.

Businessman vs. Leader

Before we begin analyzing the dynamic model, we need to clarify the difference of being a businessman or a leader. These are two distinctive social roles, in that being a businessman does not also make you a leader and vice versa. **These roles have different requirements** and, as a consequence, they demand for different knowledge, skills, abilities, and other personal characteristics (KSAOs) (Frese & Gielnik, 2014).

If you want to undertake both roles you first have to consider whether you possess all the qualities for both of them. If not, then you should appoint someone else to do the things at which you are not very good. Becoming a businessman means that you are willing to undertake the risk that comes with that decision, especially in the beginning when the costs and the uncertainty may never be compensated for. But if you also want to manage your business, you have to become a leader which means that you need some soft skills such as openness to new ideas, conscientiousness, emotional stability (stress tolerance), and extraversion (Frese & Gielnik, 2014).

However, the most important skill of yours should be to recognize the skills of others, and then stand by them, support them to bring out the best in their selves. You have to recognize their personal feelings, and their aspirations and try to help them personally develop while accomplishing the common purpose. In other words you need to **reconcile the personal with the collective**.

I clarify the conceptual meaning of these two professional titles, because they are **two distinct social roles with a significant impact on people's wellness and society's prosperity**. Being either a businessman or a leader (or both), you are responsible to deliver your own role tasks, plus you have the responsibility of other people, to set the right context for them to deliver their roles. Whatever you decide to be, do it consciously and conscientiously.

Disambiguation: Being a leader not a Pharaoh

I found myself once in a discussion with a leadership coach. He was telling a story about his intention to advise a CEO he was coaching to sit in his C-Chair and visualize the future of his company. Then someone else, who would be well-paid, would take over all the hard work of implementing the CEO's plans.

Well, this is not leadership, this is "Pharaonism". Your people will be doing the work because you pay them, but leadership is about making them believe in your dreams. And they will totally devote themselves to your plans when they see you working with them for their realization, not just sitting in your "throne" pretending to be someone special. You are not special, you are just different with different knowledge and competencies. You need to combine your strengths to make something big, something that matters.

"There are no special people, just people with specialties"

Antonis Gavalas

Interdependence & Diversity

Don't look for your reflection in your people

At the very core of organizational existence is the fulfilment of a higher strategic goal, purpose or vision. No man can make it alone, however, and this is the reason societies were created in the first place (West, 2004). We need each other to complement our weaknesses. The same stands for businesses and organizations. People with diverse backgrounds are combining their KSAOs for an optimal outcome. In the same way an organization invests in and develops its technological equipment, it also has to invest in its people and further develop their KSAOs.

Businessmen and managers who do not act as leaders make a major mistake. They are trying to find in their people the reflection of their own thoughts, perceptions, and understanding about the environment and how things should be working. But the only thing they manage is to replicate what is already possessed. They lose the opportunity of new ideas and, imprisoned in the same context, they never grow, instead they collapse under their own vanity. It's like living and moving around within a closed loop, having no idea what is going on outside.

Creating a team of "sameness" blocks the flow of information and knowledge and the total team KSAOs will never grow further. Hence you lose the benefits of synergy. This is where team interdependency abides (Alper et. Al., 1998; Sargent & Sue-Chan, 2001). We need each other's strengths to fill our own gaps and weaknesses and grow as a group beyond our restricted individual capabilities. This is why **a leader's mind-set and behavior must be neither restricted nor**

restrictive. It should be inclusive, open to different approaches and perspectives.

An organization is an independent living organism that must grow its own thinking, relieved from any kind of personalized culture emanating from its leader/founder's personality, and personal ambitions. **An organization is an entity with a given role in the society**, and should be developing an open system receptive to new data, in order to constantly be expanding by absorbing new knowledge, and then even creating its own by aiming to innovation.

Don't try to make your people think as you do, don't try to mirror your own personality. Utilize their unique KSAOs and discover new opportunities, do not be afraid of the different and the innovative, even if it seems hard to be done or even irrational. **Create a sound culture that supports the interdependence through diversity**, a culture that generates active communication and evaluates new ideas. Diversity is the only way to ever growing success.

You are playing on the same team, having different interdependent roles, equally important for the collective success. You are there for them, and they are there for you. Ask for their opinion, ask for their help as well. *Listen and ask more than you tell and impose*. Show your interest in and trust their abilities, it will make them feel important. People like that feeling, it is motivating.

Innovation as a new management approach

Innovation does not only apply in products and services. It could also be a competitive advantage in an organization's management system. There are positive consequences for the organization, also positively affecting its customers in the long term, since increased efficiency and effectiveness generate positive emotions of satisfaction, harmony and performance (Barrick et al., 1998). But the result is also practical by offering better services and products at the time customers need them.

Innovation in management systems means that the organization learns to adapt to an ever changing environment, and we know that **in nature only the organisms that adapt are finally surviving through excelling development in relation to competition** (Cookson, 2013). For that the organization must develop a dynamic system with all hierarchical levels being free and able to read the environment and suggest changes in order to follow and even being ahead of the markets' demands. We are talking about **a self-organized system balancing between standardization and adaptability** (Boulton & Allen, 2007). Standardization refers to the short-term stability, and adaptability to the long-term adjustment to the new environmental data.

In other words, an organization should have established and well-functioning processes but also the capability to detect new trends and new opportunities in the market, and rapidly respond accordingly. You do not need a restrictive management system, but a system that is free to organize itself. This is immediate and time effective. For that you need to delegate authority in decisions, have open communication channels, develop trust, give space for individual initiatives, and leave your people utilize and combine their skills in an effective manner (McDonald & Keys, 1996). In other words, **you need to let your people act freely within a commonly agreed context.**

"Keep their mind engaged,

not encaged"

Antonis Gavalas

The Garden Effect Model

Complexity theory asserts that **there is order in chaos**. Behind a seemingly random phenomenon there is a pattern of interacting factors. However, those factors are too many and mostly unpredictable, so the result seems irrational. Complexity theory makes a step further from chaos theory, trying to explain how a complex system, consisted of multiple elements, organizes itself, functions, and evolves (Dann & Barclay, 2006).

An organization is also considered a complex system with numerous interacted independent factors, resulting in **a collective behavior (phenomenon) that no individual element would express itself in isolation**. It is a living system, and as such is dictated by dynamic forces which can neither be stable nor predictable (Boulton & Allen, 2007). **Complexity theory's approach is to leave a system organize itself**. It is hypothesized that the system will be constantly changing (non-stable) and adapting itself into the environment, through a continuously learning process, in a way that will best benefit the system (McElroy, 2000).

In management, complexity theory suggests that over-control on the system should be eradicated, and replaced with a more flexible and liberal leadership approach. The environment is not explained by linear correlations between causes and effects, rendering it unpredictable (Montuori, 2009; Eisenhardt & Piezunka, 2011). *If you leave the system alone it will adjust, through a latent process of conflict and cooperation, and finally reveal its best potential.*

In a complex system like businesses, and humans themselves, you should apply the simplest possible management. **The role of leaders/managers is not eliminated, instead it is even more important and useful** (Obolensky, 2007). Their job is to set the context, the organizational purpose and main strategic goals, and then leave the system to find its own way to success. They then need to monitor the system in order to intervene if something goes astray. They need to **sustain a balance between over-organization and complete chaos**. Watch the system grow itself, just as the gardener takes care of its garden.

The **Garden Effect Model** presented here is a dynamic management system approach based on chaos and complexity theories. It brings an equilibrium within an organization through balancing its opposing dynamic forces, such as individual goals and personalities. It **promotes an optimum state between individual freedom and development and collective performance and prosperity**. It balances between freedom and control, sustaining and progressing life and avoiding destruction.

Imagine that your organization is a garden. There is no need for you to say how the flowers and the trees will grow, they know how to do it themselves. However, if you do not set the context of growing, if you do not shape your garden, it will end up looking like a jungle. This is considered as chaos. But as we mentioned above, behind this chaos there is an order, a reason why those plants grew in a certain way.

The reason is that the elements of the system (the plants) "decided" to grow in a way most fitted to their best of their existence. They actually self-organized themselves. It is still a viable organization, we just do not like how it looks. In other words it is far away from our vision of a tidy and well-shaped garden. So, the role of the gardener is exactly that, to mold the garden and watch it grow itself, intervening when there is a need for correction, to put things back on the road of the initial goal.

The same stands for organizations. If you leave people alone, they will organize themselves in an effective way that will allow them to survive, even without a specific purpose and process. **You, the leader, are their gardener**. In the beginning you design the processes and set up the system in a way that functions and grows towards the fulfilment of the organizational vision and strategies (the organization's role in the society).

People will then find their way to best function within the specific context. Then you only need to watch out for them and support them every time they lose their path, and help them get back on it. If you over-control them they will not bring out the best in them, just like a flower will not reveal its full natural beauty if you mold it within a tight frame.

This is not an easy approach, though. This theory would best work if the organization consists of people who are willing and capable of working independently and within a team without strict supervision (Obolensky, 2007). They must be motivated to undertake such responsibilities. Managers/leaders can create a learning culture and put appropriate incentives in place in order to educate their people in working within a dynamic management system as the GEM approach dictates.

Each individual should have a clear perspective of their own roles and the overall organizational purpose. Then grand them the authority to organize themselves. Complexity approach could be considered as the evolution of transformational leadership, and **it calls for higher level of organizational maturity** in terms of KSAOs and willingness for personal initiative. The purpose of this book is to present a management model that will lead your people and your processes to that level and help you create a successful organization.

Simplicity Theory

One of my core suggestions refers to simplicity in management practices which is actually dictated by the complexity theory. As mentioned above, complexity theory asserts that there is order in chaos, in that if we leave a system alone it will eventually get self-organized. The same stands for organizations. **People are complex entities** as individuals, and consequently even more complex as groups. So, **leading people requires a simple management system**. Leaders should set the main directions and the goals or the overall vision, and then leave the system alone to organize itself.

I believe we have all felt that we are more efficient if we do not have our supervisors breathing down our necks. Our thinking is more clear and creative, as well as effective, and our performance increases along with that joyful feeling of creation.

However, we don't promote anarchy, but we foster freedom of action within a predetermined and clearly set context. **We decide the "what" (we want) and "why", and leave the "how" (to do it) to our people**. If they are clear about their mission they will not go astray. Of course, they must be willing and capable of undertaking such responsibility. We, as leaders, must then stand by them and provide them with direction if they encounter any problems. They must feel our support in every step they make.

But, be cautious! Simplicity is not an easy approach, it takes careful planning to be effective. Moreover, leaders must utilize their inner thinking in order to associate information, ideas, and experience towards a systemic planning which is always open to change and development. To do that they must constantly develop their knowledge and skills, and be informed about management, social, and technological advancements. They must develop their learning capacity, and extensively study human behavior and its impact on performance. Finally they must have a holistic perspective of the world which is constantly under review and examination.

The second ramification of simplicity theory is how we evaluate our people. There are many assessment tools assessing various constructs, such as personality, leadership style, behavior etc., at the individual and the team or organizational level, using either subjective or objective measures (Cohen & Bailey, 1997; Senior, 1997; Stewart 2006) . Most of them however are sophisticated tools developed over many years of research and empirical study, rendering them overcomplicated. They measure multiple dimensions of a concept by using complicated statistical analyses.

Although those tools have a sound theoretical base and extensive empirical justification, it seems they cannot capture the whole range of human complexity. They sometimes fail to account for the variation of what they are meant to evaluate. I am not suggesting to abolish them, just not to fully rely on them when trying to transform our people. Humans are so complex that we need to use our also complex intuition in order to assess their progress after an intervention. Statistics are not capable (yet) of fully representing people's functioning. **People can be counted in numbers, but cannot be explained by numbers**.

When assessing your people: think simple, use simple measurements or/and construe sophisticated assessment tools in a simple way. Use measurements as a starting point to commence a transformational discussion. Your people's progress, development, and actual performance will then be apparent in their everyday behaviors/actions, not within worksheet cells full of numbers.

Assessment tools are great for setting the context, and providing direction. After that you should mostly rely on your observations about progress and overall contribution to the organization. Tools just come to your aid. Remember that **you cannot assess a complex system, such as humans, by using an also complex assessment system**.

Follow a simplistic approach based on complexity's qualities. Remember that there is a rationale behind the mess. People will grow in a way that fits to their development, depending on the environment. But bear in mind that **setting an organizational context is an environmental factor itself**. The only thing you need to do is to give initial direction. If they have a specific direction they will develop within that context, by finding the most effective way for their growth, and they will do it in a way that will benefit the organizational purposes as well. The individual will grow within and along with the collective. People will move around, they will observe, they will learn from each other and accordingly they will adapt their actions and their behaviors in order to complete their tasks. **That is the model of tomorrow, an ever learning and ever growing living system**.

Just do not rush, you need to be patient because it takes time for them to find their way. A learning organization takes time to reach the relevant maturity level of their elements (i.e. processes, people, and resources). Educate your people, support them along the way, and help them each time they need it. Don't throw them in the middle of the ocean. You first need to teach them how to swim, to let them get used to the water and what is under the surface. There is a stepwise process before you stop holding their hand. Below you can find some statements you need to rate your organization's maturity.

1. People master their tasks

2. People have all the resources and autonomy they need

3. People can collaborate effectively

4. People are trustful and honest

5. They have the motivation to perform and succeed

6. They have the knowledge

7. They are open to learning

8. They actively listen

9. They can collectively make decisions

10. They accept responsibility for their decisions

11. They are not afraid to make mistakes and know how to correct them

12. They act like entrepreneurs within the organization

13. They care about quality and satisfy internal customers

14. They are supportive

15. They are conscientious

16. They can handle their emotions and the emotions of others

17. They invest energy and time

18. They are ambitious and visionary

19. They know when and how to ask for help

20. They are reliable and accountable

If you rate your people highly on these statements (*use a 1-10 scale*), you have probably reached a high level of organizational maturity. If not, turn those statements into "why" and "what" questions and find the reason and the actions you should take to change the situation. A system will probably not be ready from the beginning to act alone. You first have to set the directions (context), the clarity of roles, and the awareness of the relational dynamics. Then the system, as a living organism, **has the ability to learn from its own experience**, and as the time goes by it will become more mature, and able to act more and more on its own.

Think of yourself when you are working. In the beginning you may have checklists and written processes in front of you (context). As you become familiar with the job and learn from your own experience, you need the "manuals" less and you act more freely and are able to be more flexible in your decisions. Of course the usefulness of the processes does not ware out. You always visit them when you have doubts or do not remember something. They are there to re-direct you when things are not working as predicted or expected.

Not Losing the Meaning of Life

Complexity theory has nothing to do with the complex world we are living in. Complexity refers to causes and effects and how they are interrelated, a naturally inherent phenomenon. **Our complex world is an artificial life style**. Many authors, many academics and researchers, and many practitioners are trying to come up with models of how to cope with our complex world. Why not just trying to make the world simpler? We are making our societies, and we can opt to make them complicated or simplified. See the big picture as humanity – how can something that waits for you to be created be constantly ahead of you? **It's like chasing our own tail**. We can set the pace.

Technology is another oxymoron phenomenon. We are creating technology to make our life easier, and we can actually do more with less effort. But, technology is making our life more complex than it can simplify it. Isn't that weird? We create a crazy and hysterical world, when we just need to find a way to ease complexity by just creating simplicity. After all, we need to find purpose, not to lose the meaning of life, and most importantly not to lose life itself. **Before humans comes humanity, before success comes happiness**. You don't want to be successful and miserable.

"Create an inter-independent environment, in which people need each other to complete their tasks, while they are still retaining their free-minded autonomy to utilize their full potential and personally grow along with the organization."

Antonis Gavalas

Model Integration

The dynamic model (the GEM) I present is based on the complexity theory, expanded to a simplicity approach. By reading this book, you will learn how to build an organization of freed people. **A free-minded organization needs free-minded people**. The same stands for open minds. You will achieve that by **creating a living organism which is moving on simplified (less) system lines**. The simpler the model the better. It is well known and followed by scientists that between two models that fit equally well to a concept (or that are equally effective), we follow the parsimonious way and opt for the simpler one (Stewart, 1993). We need to constantly think about how to simplify management systems. One way to do this is by providing people with more and more autonomy.

An organization will not be able to immediately put in practice an innovative management system that calls for less restrictive rules and processes, and less supervision. It will need to follow the "maturity" steps. Regarding the complex environment and competition, **urgency is good for promoting change, but change is better accepted if made in small steps and unobtrusively**. Moreover, there will be less resistance if you let the system change itself. The opposite creates opposition and change might fail (Strebel, 1996). But there is a strong explanation behind that phenomenon. We, humans, are not good at absorbing new information fast, we lack the capacity for that. We need time, focus, energy, and self-motivation (Kahneman, 2011).

Unfolding the model, you need to create the appropriate context (environment) that fosters and enables organizational dynamics to their full potential. Such an environment should provide clarity of roles, processes and expectations, and relationships development. Interpersonal relationships are also an environmental factor affecting cooperation and performance. Once these are secured, the next step is to let your people enough "space" to find opportunities (within the organization) for personal and professional development. This is the motivational factor that will keep the engine running and speeding up. You need a supportive leadership for that, and appropriate resources. People who can see their future within the organization will be more engaged. You should ask your people how they would like to contribute based on their abilities (if they cannot do it, they will not do it), and interests.

The ultimate goal of a liberal dynamic management model is to create accountable people who will also act as entrepreneurs of their roles (ownership). Lead them forward by letting them make decisions, applying their own ideas, and asking what they need to successfully deliver. **Leaving your people free to act according to their capacity means that they will at least put as much effort as they need to be successful in order to survive within the organization**. It's our instincts leading us to that directions. Then the minimum performing ability will be set. After and above that, there will be some people in your organization with enough aspirations to go to the next creational stage and level of effectiveness. They will try to excel their own instinctive survival approach and go for new fields of higher achievements to their own and their organization's benefit. Then a new culture will be created, strong enough to inspire everyone else to follow.

Nothing in nature stays stable. We can see that everything is dictated by dynamics, even teams and organizations. Building a dynamic management system based on the GEM means that you will create a learning organization, able to **change and adapt by reading the**

environmental factors and trends. It will also have adequate levels of stability since processes and responsibilities will be in place. Your freed elements (people) of that system will be able to flexibly decide in every instance by using their skills and their team knowledge capacity. Change will be easier, continuous and effective within a liberal system of increased autonomy and less supervision. You just have to prepare the right context.

"Perfection is the drive,

not the result"

Antonis Gavalas

Story: The Entrepreneur

Speaking of a dynamic system, we perceive it as susceptible to change, consisted of moving parts. **Humans are indeed "moving parts", in space and in behavior**. I recall a memory from the age of 18, even before I started studying management. I was waiting in a queue at a public service, and I remember this entrepreneur talking on his mobile phone with one of his employees. He was speaking loudly, and I kept one phrase that shaped my beliefs about entrepreneurship. The phrase was *"you do nothing right when I am not around"*.

Of course Mr. Businessman, they do nothing because you never set the context for them to be able to do something. You want to have everything under your control and your decision. That approach will never train your people in decision-making, because they do not have the autonomy they need to be flexible and act effectively. Don't be afraid of their mistakes. After all, you make wrong decisions as well. **Don't let perfection limit your way, let it drive your way**. As humans we cannot avoid making mistakes, but we can learn from them. Our willingness to reach perfection is what moves us forward. It's our motive to keep on trying and progressing. We get close but we do not touch it, and this is our incentive. If we were perfect, we would be something else, not humans, and who knows, this could be boring. Humanity needs its imperfection in order to keep advancing as much as it needs death in order to value and propagate life.

As we described above, in complexity and simplicity theories, the system is complex. Your people will know how to act, according to your strategic plan, if you have clearly set your expectations. Unless you do so, the system will fall into anarchy, doing what fits best for it to grow, which might be different from your vision of your own "garden". Just don't forget to sustain a simple structure so the movement of the system's elements (i.e. people and processes) is easier, clearer, and hence more efficient. A free system that liberates people's movement, literally and intellectually/behaviorally, will become a self-learning and self-growing system, taking advantage of its own obtained experience. Its parts (people) will result in the optimum balance for achieving growth within the context that you have explicitly set.

Developing Roles

In this section of the book I will provide you with tools that will practically help you build a high performing organization, based on the concepts of complexity and simplicity theories we have discussed so far to build our liberal dynamic management model, the Garden Effect Model.

Whatever you do, it is most important that you first clarify the characteristics of each role. **We work in teams and we have to be aware of our responsibilities, but also about the responsibilities of others**. Defining each one's roles enables the most effective utilization of diversity. It's the beginning of understanding each other's difficulties and needs. We can then better support each other to the benefit of the many (Partington & Harris, 1999).

Defining roles is one of the core determinants of team/organizational performance. There is no sense to be making any effort to improve performance, if it's not clear who does what. People need to be clear about what they are doing (Schermerhorn et al., 2003). It fosters better relationships, and builds the foundation of an effective cooperation. People will not be feeling they have contradicting roles, and the inter-role conflicts will be minimized (or eliminated) resulting in less interpersonal conflicts.

Furthermore, brain science has offered even more proof that **we humans are not multitaskers**. Our brain works in a parsimonious way, saving energy, focusing it on one task at a time (Epstein, 1984; Cookson, 2013; Houdè, 2013). You need to switch before moving on to a new task. So, people need to know exactly their roles and focus their energy there. Focus will make them better and motivate them. If roles are vague and you expect from them to do pretty much everything, they will never perform as much as you would like them to. Define each role's main characteristics and set clear expectations. You also need to delegate the appropriate autonomy level, because **a free mind is a better mind**. Follow the garden effect, be the gardener, and let your people as free as they can take, and they will prosper.

Clarity eliminates fear of the unknown, people don't see it as a threat to avoid it, and readily commit to it since they understand how they can contribute to the team/organization. This rationale does not come in contradiction to prosocial behavior (Borman, et al., 2001). People should still offer their help, beyond their main responsibilities, but they have to **be clear about what is officially expected from them, and what they are evaluated for**. Stress levels are significantly decreased with clarity, and people perform better when they are emotionally stable. Many suggest stress-relieving techniques, such as meditating, but be cautious. These techniques mostly cover the symptoms of stress (and burnout); they don't eradicate its causes. Most probably you will need to rethink about your context, processes and culture.

This first tool comes to your aid in improving communication, and engagement. Use the form below to list the roles and their requirements, what resources have to be in place, the scope of their decision making (autonomy levels), who communicates with whom, and finally how each role contributes to the organizational goals. This tool also helps in creating the process flow.

Role Definition

Role Description	Tools & Resources	Decision autonomy	Communication channels		Contribution to goals (expectations)
			Report to	Report from	

Role Impact

At the very core of all roles is interdependency. That is why we assign roles in the first place, because no one person alone can effectively and efficiently finish an integral task. So, by definition the existence of roles create interdependent dynamics, in that the one affects the other in the chain of processes. As the work flows through phases and roles, there are many things that can affect each role. We need to be aware of these effects, how they work, what their impact is, and what we can do to improve performance (flow).

Understanding the impact will let you and your people manage your behavior and actions in a way that will benefit cooperation and collective performance. Recognize these collaboration points (where actions of one meet actions of the other) and you will have a clear image of what you could do better and what to avoid. Awareness and vigilance increase focus of effort, resulting in better cooperative relationships.

The Garden Effect Model

Role	

Affects *(Other roles or processes)*	How	Impact	What to do better	What to avoid

Affected by *(Other roles or processes)*	How	Impact	What to do better	What to avoid

"People are difficult to change, but you can always change the context"

Antonis Gavalas

Personal Characteristics

Our personality determines much of our behavior, consisting of multiple traits which are well rooted in our psychosynthesis (Barrick & Mount, 1991). There is much discussion on whether we can change our behavior or not. Theoretically we can, but it is so difficult that it seems practically impossible. However, behavior may change within different contexts. For instance, an impatient individual may calm down and make things in a slower pace, if the organizational culture dictates as such. That is why **we look into behavior not as an isolated concept but as an interrelated system**. Clarifying the term culture, is nothing more (or less) than the collective behavioral expression that is created by the interacted dynamics of the people comprising this culture. In other words, it is the outcome of the interrelationships of all personalities together.

Don't forget that culture is "dynamic", meaning that it can change through time, and after focusing a substantial amount of effort on it. We can compare the discussion of personality and cultural change to the discussion about the chicken and the egg. A loop is created, and we reasonably wonder "do personalities change culture or does culture change personalities?" In fact, the question is non-existent. There is no evolutional support. The order is clear, the chicken was created evolutionally, and then after growing a reproductive system the egg came out. It's the same with people and cultures. We need to create or recreate ourselves, as individuals, and then we can broaden the change onto a collective, cultural level. So, the point is that we have to look into the unit, change ourselves (or control ourselves), and then turn our **focus onto how we can co-exist as social beings with relational norms and values**.

The following tool will guide you to analyze your core personality traits. You will have the opportunity to see how you see yourself and how others see you. You will then be able to think and change your awareness about your behavior. After revealing the "personal", then as a team you will have a clear image about the dynamics of your interpersonal relationships, how they are created, and how they can be recreated in order to transform your organizational culture. Just be honest!!

You can always use one of the many personality tests which are based on different taxonomies, but we need to keep it simple. Use your everyday language skills to describe yours and others' personalities. You know them and you know yourself, so you can tell something about them. At this stage you don't need a sophisticated and probably complicated tool. You only need your observations about yours and others' most manifested behaviors in diverse situations you experience. You need to keep it simple, you have the answers.

Tips: try to describe where the energy comes from and how someone communicates (e.g. introvert, extrovert), how s/he reacts to situations (e.g. neurotic, emotionally stable), how s/he makes decisions (e.g. rational, based on feelings, intuitively), how s/he understands the world through senses. *Some more*: assess active listening, openness to ideas, learning style, conscientiousness, teamwork, supportiveness etc.)

Describe you own personal behavioral characteristics	
See what others have to say about you	
See any differences?	
What are you going to do to close the gap (towards getting better as a person and as a team player)	

What are the assets	How can you utilize them within the team
What are the vices	How can you mitigate them – make better

Formal Factors

Relational Dynamics

Relational dynamics are affected by many factors, controllable or uncontrollable. It is very important for people who work together to be aware of those dynamics and how they are affecting their interpersonal relationships, and their personal and collective performance as well (Callaway, et al., 1985). The dimensions to be considered are the hierarchical and the role position of each person, creating **Power and Role dynamics** respectively. The important thing is to locate those dynamics by juxtaposing your role and power with those of others, and then increase your understanding of how this relationship works. You need to become aware of the difficulties each power or role comes against to, and finally reveal what the reasons that are possibly deteriorating your relationship, hence your performance, are. Then you should suggest actions that would improve that relationship, what you could do and what you would expect others to do.

Relationships must be clearly defined, so that people are not afraid of hidden agendas and politics. It is easier to allocate energy and focus your attention once you are aware of what you are looking into. Honesty, and mutual dedication towards improvement will normally increase motivation.

> TIP: don't forget to ask your people what they want to change, what doesn't work for them, how they feel about this, and what really works and they can learn from it in order to do even better.

Power Dynamics

Your Position			
Member			
Power Position			
How position (power) affects relationship			
The difficulties of your position that hinder relationship			
The difficulties of the other's position that hinder relationship			

How position (power) difficulties affect your relationship and your cooperation? (explain why relationship may not work)			
What conversations are hard to be made			
What conversations you should start to improve your interaction			
What do you expect the other to do or start			

Role Dynamics

Your Role			
Member			
Role			
How this role affects your job — Positive effects (enabling)			
How this role affects your job — Negative effects (hindering)			
Your difficulties in role that hinder relationship			
The other's difficulties in role that hinder relationship			

How role difficulties affect your relationship and your cooperation? (explain why relationship may not work)			
What you can do to improve relationship/performance			
What the other can do to improve relationship/performance			

TIP: Behaviors are difficult to change. Try to find what you can do to change the position of the relationship (e.g. move people in different positions, or separate them geographically) or the process (e.g. develop new processes, use technology etc.).

The Energetic Leader and the Lazy Follower Phenomenon

An example to understand the relational dynamics that positional (power) relationships create is the "energetic leader and the lazy follower phenomenon". We express different behaviors when the situation changes, depending on our role and our power position. Accordingly, we provoke different behaviors from others.

If we are asked to describe a leader, we will probably attribute characteristics such as energetic, hardworking, idea generator. On the other hand, our description of a follower may not be as flattering. We would probably describe them as lazy, unwilling, and uncommitted. But we have also seen that same person exhibiting the latter behavior as a follower, and the former one when that person becomes a leader. Why does this happen? What changes when we transfer from one position to the other?

To illustrate my point, let me take you on a time-trip some years ago when I was serving in the army. I served both as a soldier and as an officer, hence as a follower and as a leader. I recall a specific memory when we were running for exercise. I believe we all have an image in our mind's eye of a squad exercising, with everyone being aligned. When I was in line I sometimes felt frustrated and bored, and I was certainly feeling tired much faster. And then I became an officer and I found myself out of the line, leading the squad. The physical energy expended was much greater. I was running with my soldiers, plus I had to speak loud setting the rhythm, and putting them back to pace. Moreover, I had to run back and forth to check the back lines. All these actions required more effort, however I wasn't feeling tired at all. On the contrary, I felt full of energy, and motivated.

Why does this happen? Because as a leader you feel the excitement of leading others, the responsibility, and the joy of creating and molding others, because even as a squad leader you shape the body and develop self-discipline for your soldiers, preparing them for battle. The mere title of "Leader" creates an internal driving energy.

The same applies in the workplace between managers and their subordinates. It is easier to give orders than to follow orders. **As a leader you are free to "move" around and make decisions, and that's mind alleviating**. As a leader you can better fulfil your plans of personal development, hence your motivation is increased. As a follower, on the other hand, you usually don't know what's coming, you hang on your leader's decisions. His/her brain generates ideas, and that is an energy booster. The leader combines ideas, implements a lot of thinking and then the decision comes. As a follower, however, you are not aware of that process. You are just presented with the final decision and you have to follow, to execute the order. This is frustrating most of the times, because people tend to resist every time something new comes up. The unknown takes more effort to be understood and our brain is inherently lazy, hence the resistance. People need to understand and be motivated in order to spend and allocate their energy.

Bear all of these ideas in mind when you lead people. Be aware of their feelings and put them in the game should you want them to feel the same passion as you. You cannot put them under constant change nor make them feel the fear of the unexpected. **Share your thoughts and make the changes, but communicate their purpose first**. Give them freedom to realize some of their own ideas and make some decisions on their own. Most importantly give them the opportunity to fulfil their ambitions, to be the leaders of their own self. Then they will be more willing and motivated to follow you, and they will surely feel more energetic and vigorous. Don't forget, giving orders is easier than executing them. Don't demand things that even you are not able to deliver. Stand by your followers, lead them by example, give them direction whenever they lose it, execute with them if need be. Finally, remember that **leading is more about helping others do their jobs than them helping you do yours**.

Our relationships are dictated by our roles and our positions in the hierarchy. We act and react differently and in interdependence, composing a complex behavioral sequence which determines our co-existence, and cooperation. Mind those dynamics and you will find the tip of the Gordian knot, and along with increasing your individual and collective performance.

Resolve Conflicts – The Power of Power

Going deeper into the conversation about dynamics, **roles are attached to different power effects**. Have you noticed that? We don't feel the same emotions or consequences when the same situation happens in diverse relationship types. Take a conflict, for example. You get angry with someone, you yell, and negative impact takes place. Emotions may be the same in many relational types, but how you get out of the conflict mostly makes the difference. With a friend of yours you may find yourself involved into misunderstandings but you probably forget it quickly enough.

But with a colleague of yours things are different. Negative emotions may stay for a long time, especially when it comes to hierarchical positions. Think of your supervisor. Probably you cultivate deep and adverse emotions that you find difficult to cope with. This hinders your relationships, and your performance. *Reluctance to openly communicate the problem is probably the cause perpetuating and increasing the problem itself.*

There are many people that we find difficult to communicate openly with, because they exert some kind of power on us, even if they are not our supervisor, but just a random person we meet. It may be due to fear, to respect (e.g. an elder), to submission etc. The fact is that we have to be aware of it, and our feelings, when this happens, and try to understand the relational circumstances this power creates. Then we may find the way to resolve the situation.

The following tool will help you reveal those dynamical differences between different types of relationship. Once you become aware of them, it will be easier for you to accept the situation, and further analyze it and resolve it. Acknowledging that each relationship has its difficulties may also alleviate the burden. Furthermore, you may get some good ideas by comparing different situations and learn from each one separately on how you should probably react. Finally, it will help you start the appropriate discussions with the person of interest.

Describe the instance			
Who do you have the problem with?			
Role		Position	
What is your power relationship	Can you communicate openly?		Are you afraid talking about sensitive issues?
What are your feelings about the situation?			
What do you do about it (your reaction)?			
Is your response effective? Why? (learn from your answer)			

Imagine you are going through the same situation with another person		
	Name him/her	How would you deal with the same situation? *Describe your feelings and your (re)actions*
Supervisor		
Subordinate		
Peer		
Friend		
Family		
Spouse		

Come back to the person you have the problem with. What will you do to resolve the situation?	
What would you expect him/her to do?	
How do you plan to start the discussion and what are you going to say (key words/subjects)?	

Taking the Risk

You need to use the power of power in order to understand your relational dynamics and improve your cooperation and productive conflict. People have to find what hinders their open conversations with other people, and resolve or remove those blocks. Destructive conflicts or avoidance of conflicts do not move things (and relationships) forward (West, 2004). Fight or secrecy just make the situations worse. You need to ask your people how they feel when something comes up, how they approach the situation (their perspective in terms of beliefs and interests), what they need in order to resolve any dissonance, and what their fears are that are not letting them find peace and/or solution within their own self.

Relationships are not easy. **We cannot fit with every human being and not all human beings can fit with us**. However, we are talking about a dynamic system, which means that nothing is stable but susceptible to change. By "change" we mean people may change and processes may change, or other environmental factors may change. It takes time to build an optimally high performing group of people (Sargent & Sue-Chan, 2001; Harrison et al., 2002). Everything is fluid and flows. We have to take the risk with relationships.

Don't create your opinion in haste when it comes to judging people. You may be wrong. **People are tested under multiple and diverse circumstances before we can conclude about their personality**. Don't be afraid to take the risk with people in all aspects of your life. You may be hurt or betrayed, but when you find the right people around you it is worth the cost. Most importantly, **do not get disappointed**. You will have to invest in human relationships as you invest in machines for your production line. People are part of your business process, and they are your most valuable assets. As you know, investments come with risks. Sometimes you lose but other times you win. Winning in that case is long-term relationships, and they are worth it.

Saying "No"

You expect people to be honest, to openly express their opinion and state that something is not right or that they made a mistake that needs to be corrected. But **you do not understand your power over them**. Yes, some people, sometimes regardless their position, exert a power over others who in turn feel intimidated and are not willing to speak freely. You have to leave some space for them to say "no", to assertively oppose and have their perspective expressed.

I am not implying a "viva la revolution" approach, we don't actually have to start a coop to say what we believe. People just have to be able to express themselves. Otherwise you will lose a lot of good ideas, opportunities for improvement, and make mistakes that you could have otherwise avoided. I remember reading about teams working under adverse conditions (Rosnet, et al., 2004; Schmidt, et al., 2004; Steel, 2005). There were occasions in aviation were plane crashes happened only because the second pilot didn't have the courage (or the confidence) to express his own opinion to the first pilot (Helmreich & Merritt, 2000; Flin et al., 2002; Nullmeyer & Spiker, 2003; Caldwell, 2005).

What you simply need to do is to:

- Frequently ask the opinion of others.

- Don't just ask and reject, but honestly consider.

- Apply their suggestions (if you believe they are right) and let them know you did so (this will increase their confidence).

- Don't cut their wings when they say something wrong or irrelevant. It doesn't matter. This is how ideas progress.

- Be polite when you don't believe they are correct, and clearly explain why.

Know Each Other More

As you can probably see, after analyzing your roles and relational dynamics you have succeeded something very important, to know each other better. This will help you increase your communication and your common understanding about the work flow and the created interdependencies. You have understood who you have to communicate with, what information to exchange, each other's difficulties, and what you can do to improve your dynamics. Now you go even deeper in your relationships. Understand their personality, their unique characteristics that bring into the team. The purpose is to recognize that we are different with diverse qualities which potentially make your team different from competition (Hogan & Holland, 2003; Mohammed & Angell, 2003). Maximizing your synergy depends on how you make use of complementing strengths, your team's diversity.

Knowing each other increases our potential for collaboration and fairness. The act of caring about people's interests and problems is perceived as an act of good will, receiving also positive behaviors (Borman, et al., 2001; Tracey et al., 2001; Markey et al., 2003). Furthermore, having all the information about your people will make you treat them fairly, either in regard to their contribution or difficulties within the professional environment or in regard to the specificities in their personal life that may affect their behavior and performance at the work place.

Just keep in mind that revealing someone's personality takes time and effort. It is said that we tend to shape our opinion about someone during the very first seconds of our acquaintance. Worse than that is the fact we abide by that impression. But, as we know, humans are prone to mistakes, because they don't take time to appropriately gather and process information, and for that it is difficult to change their impressions (Kahneman, 2011). That's why people care so much about their image, and they can easily send manipulative messages, based on well-known shared stereotypes. Other people usually buy that.

Human personality and respective behavior are too complex to be manifested during the short time of just some seconds. Your need to **observe and "test" behavioral tendencies under multiple circumstances** before you can more securely conclude about someone's personal traits. Haste will make you misjudge good and capable people, and lose a prosperous cooperation or relationship, or leave yourself exposed and vulnerable to fraud. Don't listen to what they say about our first impression being correct. It can't be, and if it can, only a few people are capable to trust their "intuition". Do you reckon you are one of them? Maybe you are, but think twice before you say you are.

Use the following tool to improve your awareness for each member of your team/organization. It will increase your ability to fully utilize them, by knowing what they can and are aspired to do. You will also support them in their difficulties, and they will feel they are treated fairly, and they are important parts of the group. In turn, they will be more committed. It is vital to analyze the context, and how the environment affects people's contribution and other behavioral expressions.

There is a dynamic mutual reaction between people and their environment, the one affecting the other. You need to know if the context lets your people reveal their full potential. Environment refers to the "habits" of working and the norms, the processes, the values, the available resources, the communication channels, the opportunities it provides, and other contextual factors potentially affecting behaviors. Find out what you can change to create the circumstances that will enable people's development and performance.

Member			
Studies	Expertize/ experience	Ambitions/ Interests	What needs to be developed
What KSAOs contribute to the team and how			
	At Work		In Personal Life
Difficulties the member encounters			

Detect the Fit
Detect other environmental or cultural factors affecting behavior
What changes can be made to improve

Informal Factors

Sympathy

There are several factors that may affect performance, other than the ones created by the organizational structure, such as roles and processes. One of the two I present here is sympathy amongst people. We choose the people we want around us according to how much we like them (Bowers et al., 2000). Likeness is determined by many subjective factors, such as appearance, behavioral expressions, beliefs and values, knowledge and expertise. We generally like to come closer to people with whom we like to communicate or develop some kind of relationship for some or all of the above reasons. As a consequence, **we don't express the same sympathy levels to everyone**.

Within our working context, we have to cooperate with people regardless of how much we like them as persons. We need to communicate, to be related just because our roles are interdepended and we need each other to complete our tasks. This is a very important factor affecting working dynamics. It is difficult to be aligned with someone you don't like and you have trouble communicating and cooperating with. If people do not get along, and their interrelated performance is affected, you could either rearrange processes (roles) and people or you could build a predictable and standardized working frame (i.e. procedures) that would be easy for those people to do their interrelated work. Technology could also significantly help people's relationships and cooperation, for example by helping their communication flow.

Likeness Matrix

In order to detect the possible existence of collaboration deficiencies due to people's likeness levels use the following matrix. Rate from 1-10 how much they like each other. If the rate is low for a pair of people, use the next table to reveal the reasons, and find effective solutions.

	Member 1	Member 2	Member 3	Member 4	Member 5	Member 6
Member 1						
Member 2						
Member 3						
Member 4						
Member 5						
Member 6						

Member		Member	
How their relationship is negatively affected?			
What is the impact at work?			
Find out specificities: describe what and how is affected in terms of tasks and processes			
Make a plan on how you can make changes to improve (e.g. change spatial factors, change roles, create standardized procedures that would minimize contact etc.)			

Emotions

Neuroscience, the science that examines at the molecular level how our brains act and react to the environment, has found sound evidence about how emotions are catalyst for positively motivating people. Emotions increase our attention, and focus towards respective action. Emotions also activate learning capacity, a vital dimension for personal development, hence increasing commitment to high performance (Kandel, 2008; Kandel et al, 2011; Houdè, 2013).

If you are willing to be a true leader of your people you need to acknowledge the power of our emotions. People need to feel satisfied and important, and in turn they become more productive, they are open to learning new things, they are team players, and supportive. The most important incentive is the feeling of recognition, and inclusiveness in the organizational development (Barry & Stewart, 1997; Tarricone & Luca, 2002; Schermerhorn et al., 2003; West, 2004). They need to feel part of it before they become more engaged.

Learn about your people's feelings, how they react, what they need in order to feel part of the team, and what they need to feel rewarded. Bear in mind that rewards motivate more than punishments (Kahneman, 2011). Thinking about the new generation, it is well-evidenced by numerous studies that money is not the only thing that generates people's engagement, and devotion. In fact, it appears lower on the list of internal incentives, with actions like autonomy, recognition, inclusiveness, and model leadership appearing as top rankers.

For a specific situation follow this tool:

Situation under examination				
Member	Describe Feelings	Reactions		How to feel better
		Negative	Positive	

Now use this tool to reveal whether each member is feeling part of the team, and what each one needs to be feeling appreciated.

Member	Rate Feeling of Inclusiveness (1-10)	What is needed to feel part of team	What they need to feel appreciated

(Re)Design your Processes

Up to now we have worked on defining roles and personal characteristics. You now have a clear view of the dynamics created. You have clarified the roles and their requirements, you developed a deep understanding about your people's personal characteristics, strengths and weaknesses, and you also know about the effects their interactions have (depending on role technicalities, personal traits, and positional relations).

The next step is to think of the work flow. You must put everything in place according to their dynamic interaction (roles and people). Think of the following and design your processes, the place of each role in the work flow. **Put the right people in the right place in relation to their KSAOs and to their interpersonal impact**. Give importance to the human interactions and locate the core nodes of your work flow, which need more focus or are more risky than others. Reassign responsibilities accordingly, taking any limitation into account. For example you cannot assign marketing tasks to an IT specialist but you may relocate roles within the IT department. But most of all, **link people's personal interests and ambitions to roles and organizational purposes**. Personal interest increases focus and motivation for performance.

This is the stage where you integrate all the work you have done with your people within you team/organization. The simplicity approach has been presented here. You need to find clear organizational systems, easy to understand and practice, in order to manage a complex system. It is not an easy task and you will probably have to try different combinations before you reach an optimized level of cohesiveness and performance. The dynamic system approach I suggest is, of course, not the only one available to adopt. I encourage you to enrich your knowledge by reading about diverse management systems and leadership philosophies. Create your own combination of tools to help your organization, and learn from the process. The key is to keep the simplest possible model that will bring the highest level of performance. This will give you the opportunity to be adaptable, and receptive to change. **Keep on the road of nature**.

Following the GEM, liberate your system taking one step at the time. Support your people to create a learning environment where they will be able to work more and more freely as they gather experience. Set the initial directions (context) and let them grow themselves.

HINT: Design the process on a paper so you can have an image of it. It will help your perspective.

Use the following table to assign or reassign roles. In role definition you have set the contribution expectations. Here be more specific of how the success or effectiveness of each role will be measured (Key Performance Indexes).

(Re)Assigning Roles

Member	Role	KPIs

Create a flow chart according to your previous work, and visualize where each role stands in relation to others within the process. In order to optimize the process, you need to investigate any potential risks or setbacks regarding the dynamic interactions between role specificities and interpersonal relationships (again considering your previous work in this book).

Are there any setbacks?

Role	Potential Risk or Setback

Now that you have located potential risks or problematic areas, analyze whether they are caused by role technicalities or human interactions (behavioral-based). Then try to proactively fix it by making changes in the work flow, always considering the implication of other roles or role holders (members) and how the interactive relationships (and cooperation) are affected by or affect the process.

Role		Role Holder	
Role-based Problems		Behavioral-based Problems	
Other roles – people implicated			
How can we do improvements	Change responsibilities within the role		
	Assign role to other (who)		
	Change place on the process flow		

Tips

o Change roles between people who can deliver and can work together more effectively. Don't forget to ask them if they really like it, and feel confident to do it.

o Create different combinations of people and roles, until you find the most effective ones.

o Rearrange the working space if need be.

o Provide your people with the appropriate resources and technology. Delegate enough authority to make decisions regarding their work that will help them successfully complete their tasks.

o Don't be afraid to make a mistake. If something doesn't work, change it again. Think of it as a team sport game.

o Clarifying roles and responsibilities takes the fear factor out of the equation, because people know what they are doing, with whom they interact, and what is expected from them. The unknown creates insecurity and fear, and human reaction is negative and/or defensive. We perceive the unknown as a threat and we resist to it, we disengage and we cannot commit to something we are afraid of.

HINT: let people contribute their own creativity, let them find their own way of working and cooperating together. That means they can make decisions to act and rearrange the system according to their interpersonal dynamics and the messages they take from the environment. You can use the tools to help you try different organizational structures, but you should also let your people do it for themselves. They will collaborate in a way that best benefits the system and their personal interests.

Liberating the System

You have now set the right context of a dynamic management system. You have clarified the roles, you have developed your awareness of the human contributions, and you have designed the actual process of your work. Everything should be in place by now and functioning effectively. You have achieved the required level of understanding and commitment. Now you have to take the next step to a fully free system according to the Garden Effect Model, which is in turn based on complexity theory. The approach however should be based on simplicity. **The fewer the supervision lines the better for the system which will be functioning based on its own dynamics**. Hence, the more liberal the merrier. Letting the system free requires total engagement and continuous learning by your people.

There is only one way for you to achieve it. **You need to take their interests and turn them into contributions**. Turn their interests into profitable assets for the organization. By profitable I don't mean immediate monetary gains. It could refer to systemic improvements, product development and many more. Consider your people as internal entrepreneurs, and their role as an internal autonomous business unit.

First, you need to connect their interests with the organizational scope and goals. That will provide purpose to their efforts. Personal goals and purpose are the ultimate motivators, fostering positive emotions and energy focus, which in turn increase our willingness to learn (develop) and perform. Then, turn their interests/ideas into actionable plans that will contribute to the organizational success. Use the following tool to help you set the foundations for a truly free dynamic system, as nature dictates, and as the new era demands.

Member			
Interests/Aspirations	Anchoring Organizational Goals	How they Link (understanding their connection)

Member			
Interest/Idea	How it can contribute to organizational success	Turn it into action/plan/product

I know what you may be thinking. Not all roles or working contexts (businesses) are able to implement such a liberal system. No system is one-for-all fit. You need to keep in mind the concept that supports the suggested management system. Combine what is provided here with your knowledge and experience, search for other approaches that would fit your organization, and design your own adapted system. **Customize according to your unique circumstances.** I could not suggest anything else but to think freely, not by the book. That's the essence of dynamics.

Let's take, for example, a bank corporation. Maybe it's not feasible to fully liberate bank tellers, following a dynamic's system norms, at least not from the very beginning, but you could liberate branches to be working with increased autonomy in their decisions, according to the specific needs of the area and customers they are dealing with. Find the right people, with the right skills and personal characteristics, to lead and they will make it happen. They will consider their branch as their own business. Then, they will treat their people within the branch according to what is suggested in this book, and they will find out the way to empower and engage their teammates. Reward them accordingly but the best compensation will be to let their mind free. **Amongst all the human needs, freedom is on the top of their list.** Of course we are talking about social freedom, but its analysis lies beyond the scope of this book.

"Leadership is a LIFE choice, not a designation."

Antonis Gavalas

Enablers

Leadership

Leadership is presented as the evolution of management. Leader is the manager who goes beyond giving orders and becomes someone that inspires and let others excel in their field, and contribute to the collective. Many believe it is the most important role in the work chain. No, **it's not more important, it is just different**! We are all humans playing a part on the stage of life and society. We all have to (or potentially can) contribute something, bigger or smaller, but equally important. Remember teamwork? We all depend on others to do things we cannot, we need others to do some things better than we can, and in that way we are after improvement as humanity not as humans. Think of yourself as another part of the dynamic system that needs to find its own effective place in relation to the other consisting parts.

I bet you want to become a leader not just a (micro)manager. You imagine yourself being responsible for other people able to show them the way, assuming that you have all the qualities of the good leader. You hypothesize you are following all the knowledge about effective leadership, you believe you are the transformational type of leader who actively listens to people and is open to their ideas. But **leadership is really about practicing it, and if you like to be sure you are doing it well, you first have to be honest with yourself**. So when we are talking about an open and dynamic leadership style:

- You ask people to be creative

  Ask yourself how much creativity you can handle

- You ask people to take initiatives

  Ask yourself how much initiative you can take

- You ask your people to create ownership

  Ask yourself how much autonomy you afford to give

- You ask your people to be trustful

  Ask yourself how much vulnerable to others you can be

- You ask your people to do things

  Ask yourself if you would do it and if you are ready to "fight" next to them against adversities

These are some basic questions, but in that rationale you can find more to test yourself, how ready you are in your inside. If your answers are highly positive, then you are on the right path towards the leadership that the modern era dictates. **Mind you that willingness to be a good person does not make you one**. You have to practice what you preach. The same stands for leadership. **Thought is not a desire, in the same way that desire is not an action**. There are three mutually affected but independent behavioral stages:

1. You think you are a good leader.

2. You desire to be one.

3. And finally you are acting as one.

As analyzed in a different section of this book, being a trustful leader requires you to be honest, consistent, and supportive. Do what you honestly believe, and lead others to do the same thing.

Being Creative

Much is said about creativity and how it benefits innovation. You need a clear mind and full energy to do that. However, I have noticed a major mistake between specialists who suggest many techniques for being creative and innovative. The mistake I believe they make is that they ritualize and, as a consequence, over-contextualize creative thinking and innovation. I am a person who has made much inner search (aka introspection), contemplating about individual and social life. I know one thing is for sure – **you cannot ritualize creativity, you cannot free your mind by putting it in a restrictive context**. Creativity takes deep introspection, and most importantly random combination of ideas (De Bono, 1992; Bailey, 2007).

But how can you generate randomness if you are trying to think by using a set of systematic steps? It is restrictive by definition. Creativity needs to develop all of your brain not just part of it. **You need to train your mind to leave its own ideas travel free in time and direction within itself**. As they collide they will find their own best combination, which each time may be different depending on your needs, the situation, or neither of these. They may just come up in the surface. In other words, they will find their way to grow themselves in a way that benefits... creativity.

Does this remind you of something? It is just what is described here as a dynamic management system, the Garden Effect Model, based on complexity with a simplicity approach. **Ideas are like the people in organizations, they are the elements of your inner garden**. They also need to move freely, and grow themselves, they know how to do it best. If you need your creativity to be focused on a specific project you just have to clarify what you want, and provide your ideas with the context (the main rules) that would dictate their combinations (their relationships). Then let them free to do the rest of the work. This is how the world works out there (the universe) and in there (in our minds).

I am not implying that the techniques and models developed by many brilliant people in order to improve our creativity are wrong. They are based on sound and well-defined theories and concepts. My argument lies in their application. They are promoted as panaceas of innovative thinking, but they may miss to point that **each one of us has to find our own way to reach our creative self**. In many cases, specific techniques become a trend, and many people are trying them out. It's good to try new things, but still you need to distill knowledge and keep what fits your personal temperament.

Evaluating your Leadership Style

Leadership Style q

Following my simplicity theory approach, asserting that people are already a complex system and they must be assessed in a simple way, I developed a plain leadership assessment tool that will uncover your leadership style preference and/or practice, and will give you insight for self-development and most effectively leading your people. Its name came up accidently. As I was saving the file and willing to type the name *Leadership Style Quadrant*, I pushed the "enter" key early by mistake. However it seemed right, because "q" stands for quadrant and quick. So, its name was born. This assessment aims to give you a fast and simple way to become aware of your leadership style, and provide you with an also simple way of how you could best practice leadership in different contexts, as well as how to develop your style towards a more mature and effective leadership level.

We can find many theories approaching Leadership Style from various perspectives, intending to analyze the way someone prefers to lead people. Many of these theories examine leaders' orientation towards the task or results, and towards the people or relationships (e.g. Kantas, 1995; Schermerhorn et al., 2003). If we combine these interchangeably used dimensions, and we attempt to assign diverse leaders' behaviors, the following quadrant diagram is created. The *Leadership Style q* consists of four quadrants configured by two complementary dimensional pairs (i.e. task and results, people and relationships) and two opposing pairs (i.e. relationships and task, people and results).

In order to assess your stance as a leader, read each description and assign a grade to yourself on the respective axis. Think of how accurately each one describes your personal style/preference. After you rate yourself in all four dimensions, connect those rates in order to draw a square or rectangular, as in the example. Each quadrant represents the maturity level of your leadership style. The more the area of the square is located in the upper right quadrant the more mature is your leadership approach.

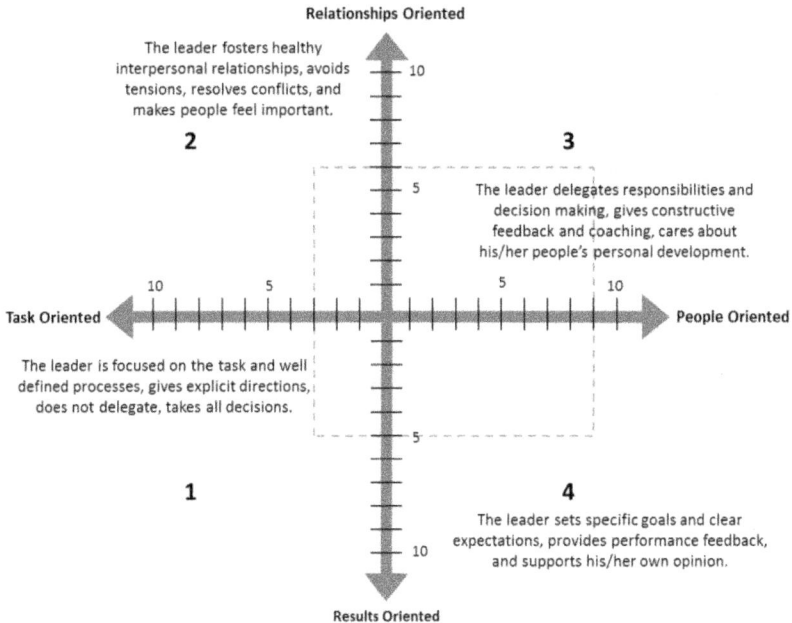

Leadership Style q

It is important to say that the development of your style as a leader also depends on the maturity of your organization and its people. If your people are not willing or cannot take responsibilities, then a more structured and directive leadership style is more appropriate. So, **our leadership style is affected by the context** we are practicing leadership within (people and processes), and by the organizational needs as well.

We cannot assert that each leadership style is more wrong or more right, but we have to create the appropriate environment in order to move towards **the third quadrant's leadership style**, the one that supports people's wellness and personal development, promotes healthy interpersonal relationships and psychological balance, while still focuses on high performance, through employee empowerment, delegation in decision making, and coaching when needed (supportive style). It takes an environment with clear organizational vision and ways of working (values) that people are committed to.

However, **at the first developmental stages** of a team/organization, it might be good to seek a style balancing between the third and the fourth or between the third and the second quadrants, where the leader cares about people and their development, gives some authority, but also sets more specific goals and gives more directions, because people are not ready yet to take full responsibility.

What if the square area moves towards **the fourth quadrant** (high results oriented and high people oriented)? It is obvious that they are mutually exclusive approaches, and you are probably confusing your people with contradictive messages. For example, you may give (or you believe that you give) authority in decision making about some things and not about others. Or you encourage decision making but you eventually give the final directions and your opinion/decision always prevails. This creates an illusion of empowerment and your people will eventually be frustrated and unmotivated.

The first quadrant style is very authoritarian and, although it might also be useful under some circumstances, it is suggested to be avoided. A first-quadrant leader is excessively domineering and creates a rigid and highly inflexible environment where people feel unmotivated, less creative, and unsatisfied. It is very likely that you lose talents and high performers.

The second quadrant leadership approach is appropriate and well-balanced for organizations comprised of people not very willing to, or that cannot, undertake responsibilities. It also fits organizations that have highly structured processes and give little space for individual initiatives and decisions as they flow (e.g. production lines, banks etc.). A second-quadrant leader cares about good relationships by fostering a supportive climate, while focusing on processes and making all decisions. However, even within a well-structured environment it is suggested that the leaders move a little towards the third quadrant style and give their people the opportunity to be creative and participate in the organization's development by freeing their thinking and making suggestions.

If the square stands in the middle it could have several explanations. You might use a little bit of each style in order to adjust to your organization's circumstances. If you lead people who need different leadership approaches, then it seems good that you can adapt to each situation and/or people. But this could also mean that organizational processes are inconsistent calling for contradictive leadership approaches each time. This needs to be addressed and resolved immediately by the leadership team. Your square standing in the middle could also mean that your leadership style is inconsistent and you are leading e.g. based on you every day mood. This also communicates incoherent messages, misleading your people and provoking great amounts of frustration. This in turn significantly lowers satisfaction and performance. You should consider revisiting your leadership beliefs and choose an appropriate style to abide with.

Think of the square area as a moving object and your leadership style as **something that adapts to each situation**. The *Leadership style q* assessment tool is a fast and simple method to gain a first insight about your behavior as a leader, and think of how your leadership style fits your organization and your people, as well as how it could be further improved.

Not a Square? Of course it is not assumed that you will get a perfect square at all times, but your results could also look more like a rectangular. In that case consider the areas at which you are very low. If you are low at the "Relationships Oriented" and/or "People Oriented" dimension, you should consider taking actions to improve them. If you are low at "Results Oriented" and/or "Task Oriented" dimensions, it could be a good thing for you to lead high self-motivated and competent people. However, if not, you should consider if the context you are working within needs a more directive leadership style. In that case, being low at those dimensions would mean that your people are not aware of what they are doing, hence their performance would also be low.

The high ends: Also be cautious if you score high on opposites. If you are high at *Relationships* you could also have high scores on each and every other dimension, it is not prohibitive. But, you should normally not score high at *People and Task* at the same time and *People and Results* at the same time. The same stands if you score high at all three dimensions at the same time (*People, Results*, and *Task Oriented*). If so, you should reconsider your leadership style. You communicate a style that is inconsistent, having a negative impact on your people's morale and performance. If you have in mind different subgroups in your organization or different ad hoc situations, meaning that you need to follow different styles in each case, then it could be conditionally acceptable. However, be cautious, revisit your leadership characteristics and image, and at all times reconsider your organizational context, in that you should examine why there is a need for you to practice different styles (this could be a call for transforming your organizational context).

Important Note

Please mind that the leadership style q assessment tool is a general approach for you to assess your preferred personal leadership style. No assessment has the ability to precisely cover all of your personal characteristics through diverse environments. We tend to behave differently depending on the context. Use assessments wisely as an aid that helps you create awareness of yourself. It would be very useful though to ask other people to assess your style by using the same four-dimensional tool. Comparing yours and others' beliefs will help you have a more accurate perception and will give you the opportunity to improve your leadership style.

The Secret of being a good leader is to see things from a human perspective. Don't think as a leader, just think as a human being who interacts with other human beings. You just have to treat them fairly and care about their prosperity by helping them find their own way to evolution.

Antonis Gavalas

Trust

Trust building lies in the very core of teamwork. Nothing of the above would work if people did not trust each other. Humans tend to imitate or correspond to others' behavior in that if you develop a trustful behavior, your people will probably reciprocate your trust (Markey, et al., 2003). They say that trust is about being vulnerable to others, not to be afraid of opening yourself and unconditionally depend on the other to do your job (Kiffin-Petersen & Cordery, 2003). But what are the determinants of trust? How can we know that trust is well-established within an organization or team? After many years of observation and literature research, and after having informal discussions with many people about what trust means to them, I ended up with three main characteristics that we may find in **a trust-based culture**. These are: honesty, consistency, and supportiveness.

Honesty

Honesty is obviously a prerequisite. This is where trust begins, in the essence of all relationships. We cannot rely on someone who does not tell the truth.

Consistency

Telling things that are true or you truly believe, either about a situation or about your beliefs and values, is not enough. Your words and actions must also be consistent. What if someone tells you that he depends on your abilities for delivering a task, but assigns the task to someone else? Of course you will think that something is not right, and you will find it difficult to trust this person again.

Supportiveness

This is the third pillar of trust. Supportiveness means that we can rely on someone to protect us whenever we need help, either when we don't know how to do something or we make a mistake, even when we are in some kind of hazard or conflict and we need protection. We said that trust is about being vulnerable to others, and we will be open to people who are being honestly, and consistently supportive.

Try to detect any trust inefficiencies, yours or others', by using the following guide. Do not hesitate to amend the table to best fit your circumstances. Of course *there is no meaning in using this tool if you are not honest to your own self*.

List things your people need from you to trust you (things you say or do)	Is what you say or do something you honestly believe?	Do you practice it under all circumstances? (*Hard times reveal true personalities*)	
Are you being supportive?	Yes / No	*Rate yourself 1-10*	
Do you tolerate mistakes, trying to help people correct them?	Yes / No	*Rate yourself 1-10*	
If some or all answers are "no" (or low rated), try to explain why			
What could you do to develop a trustful behavior?			

Communication

Communication is the means to deliver your vision, your emotions, your needs, and is the way to achieve high levels of collaboration. Communication is about transferring information and knowledge enabling the workflow, including constructive feedback. Communication must be sincere, open, and predetermined when possible (Caldwell & Everhart, 1998; Rico et al., 2008).

There are two main aspects of formal communication: the **procedural and the relational**. Procedural communication refers to well-established communication channels so everyone in the organization knows with whom and for what issues has to communicate (Gittell, 2002). Relational refers to the actual act of communicating with each other (Schermerhorn et al., 2003). It is a behavior (action) lying within each one's responsibility to express it (i.e. come in contact and communicate as appropriate). Working on your flow chart, up to now you should have a clear image of how communication channels work, according to the process flow. Use the card below for each member/role to be more specific of who is communicating with whom, and which important, formal or informal, information or knowledge they should exchange. Be specific about the method of communication (e.g. in person, by using technology etc.) and at what time intervals. Use this tool for all the possible combination of communicational pairs.

Member		Member		
Formal *information/ knowledge/feedback*				
Method and resources				
Time frame				
Informal *information/ knowledge/feedback*				
Method and resources				
Time frame				

Common Ground

(Developing Communication)

Communication would not be achievable if we didn't have a common language to communicate with. When talking about "common language" we don't mean only the grammar and syntax. **We are talking about meanings**. Words have nothing to say if we don't agree upon their meaning, what they stand for. Shared mental models are cognitive patterns that we share in explaining the world around us (Mathieu, et al., 2000). They are our common ground of communication, otherwise we could not possibly understand each other or even predict one another's behaviors, thoughts, and needs (Mohammed & Dumville, 2001). Having a common understanding enables our decision-making processes, and our collaboration (Caldwell & Everhart, 1998; Rico et al., 2008).

It is well-evidenced by neuroscience that **developing your common understanding will help you bend resistance**. Our brain has limited energy capacity, and tries to allocate it in a parsimonious way. Due to our energy saving we end up with a lazy brain, resisting to learning new things (Kandel, 2008). What usually happens is that the more familiar a concept is, the more it gets our attention, and hence it is easier for us to accept it. On the contrary, we don't readily absorb new knowledge, because the unknown causes fear which in turn stimulates our defensive mechanisms (Kahneman, 2011). We deal with what we do not understand as it would be a threat, resulting into resistance, rejection, and/or run away. So if you manage to generate a common ground of understanding through well-known concepts, it will be easier for your people to communicate openly and commit. Then you will be able to step forward and learn new things and accept new ideas more easily, without resistance.

Following our brain's economy and our vast but limited memory capacity, cultivating the frame of our shared mental models also enables us to expand our knowledge repository, by learning from each other. Our brain is limited in the number of information that can be stored or remembered, this is why we need each other to compensate for this weakness. We depend on each one's memory capacity for keeping a specific piece of knowledge. **Individual knowledge may be partial but our collective mind keeps a more complete version of it.** Having a common ground of communication is what lets us bring that knowledge together, put it in practice, and expand it even more. So, our convergent knowledge (shared concepts) enables our divergent knowledge which in turn increases our synergy (analyzed later in this book).

It is very important for teamwork to develop a common understanding. Team members will improve their **communication efficiency**, they will be able to **commit and engage**, and they will be advancing their **learning capability**. You need to locate the inefficient areas of communication that hinder your collective performance. Keep a journal of instances that generated misunderstandings, and identify the specific areas that you and others did not clearly understand. It is probably caused because of the different backgrounds, hence diverse mental models. With the following tool you will have the opportunity to converge and reconcile any communicational differences.

Journal

Write down as they occur: during a conversation or conflict/dispute locate the communication gaps, words, phrases, and concepts not well understood by you or other persons involved.

Instance	

Words, phrases, concepts you didn't understand

Words, phrases, concepts others didn't understand

Filling the Gap

Since you have located any inconsistencies in your communication ability as a team or organization, you now need to correct your shared understanding by using the following tool. Choose an instance, list what you don't commonly and clearly understand, find yours and others' perspective, and then see why you have different approaches and how you can converge them in order to improve your communication capacity and efficiency.

Instance				
Word, phrase, concept	Your understanding of it	Others' understanding of it	Mark the difference creating the problem	How can you converge?

Sharing the Same Meaning

The tools above helped you locate occurred inefficiencies in your communication processes. However, you need to prepare in advance for every task you do or subject you discuss with your people, by developing your shared understanding, and setting the right context from the very beginning for an effective and productive communication. You need to make clear what everyone should know about that task or situation, so they coordinate efficiently.

Task or Subject	
Key words or phrases everyone should know	Common understanding: explain the meaning

Development opportunities
(Ambitions & Motivation)

Role Improvement

Let your people feel and know they can develop personally and professionally. Most of us have ambitions regarding our financial or social status, our knowledge and skills. **Improvement prospects motivate people to focus and commit**. You need to know their interests, and how they aspire to grow. When people are interested in something, they willingly focus their energy (Satpathy, 2012), hence they are motivated to put more effort. Effort is the means to unfreeze your brain and learn new things. Bending brain resistance means that people are ready to change and improve by reaching new knowledge and levels of perspective (Houdè, 2013). They become receptive to new and diverse ideas, and better at collaboration.

Remember about emotions, and attention. Discuss with them the area they need to improve in, list together their strengths and their weaknesses, and co-create their development plans. **No organization grows if its parts do not grow along with it**. Actually it is the opposite that happens. Individuals grow (as units and as a team in accordance and alignment) and the organization grows accordingly.

Regarding liberating the system, and engaging people, you need to **ask them to contribute to role development along with personal development**. Since you analyze their strengths and weaknesses, and their needs or aspirations for personal improvement, you must also seek their opinion on how to implement improvement actions for their area of responsibility. This should motivate them to be accountable, master their own job, and align personal with organizational interests once again. This tool will help you create a plan of individual and team/organizational development, through training, career planning, and future human capital needs.

Member	
Area	
Strengths	
Weaknesses	
Interests	
Growth Aspirations & Plans	
Development Opportunities	
Tools & Resources	

Role Improvement Suggestions and Plans
Detailed analysis: What, rationale, who, by when, resources needed

Committed, not a Comet

Motivation is the additional value you add to a well-established work environment which is built on the pillars of Roles, Communication, and Trust (analyzed later in this book). It's like building a house. You first create a strong foundation, and then you go on adding the floors. Your people will be willing to perform and be committed to you and your organization if you provide them with a context full of opportunities, after you have secured them and made them feel free to express themselves, to contribute, to trust and be trusted. If not they will just wait until the right moment (which will be another opportunity) to leave your organization. They will just consider themselves as a comet, being around for a predetermined and probably short period of time before they "fly" to the next "solar system". If they see themselves in that way, they will never be fully committed, they will just be alert to mark their next challenge, somewhere else than your organization.

Stepwise Commitment Approach

All these four enablers, described above (**Leadership, Trust, Communication, and Personal Development**) will create the engagement level you need for everyone to embark on the journey of your collective success, i.e. fulfilling your organizational vision. A tool to further develop commitment and engagement, especially when disagreements, hidden agendas, and politics are hindering the way of a team, is the **Stepwise Commitment Tool**. The aim of this approach is to follow a targeted questionnaire as a guide to a step-by-step engagement. The questions must lead people to reach an agreement regarding as many questions/statements as possible. So, you start with a question that you know the answer will be *yes*, or at least it will be accepted by everyone in the team. You then proceed to the next possibly most accepted suggestion.

The rationale behind this tactic is to build consensus in a way that everyone will have to commit to participate and deliver a common goal (the more the merrier for team's cohesiveness). **They have to understand that, their different perspectives notwithstanding, there are things they all agree to and can work collectively to achieve them**. If you manage to secure their devotion and participation, as time progresses, they will learn how to cooperate and see that it is possible for them to collaborate effectively for the team's benefit, especially when successes start to happen. If they understand and find their common ground, it will be easier for them to accept change, and teamwork. They will see benefits and opportunities, not threats. Hence, their motivation will progressively increase.

You can use the following general guide and amend/add as appropriate according to your unique circumstances (people and situations). As you can see, in the first question if someone answers *no* there is no reason for him/her to be in the team. So, even if they "have" to give an affirmative answer, that means they are engaged by Step one.

1. Do you want our team/organization to be successful?

2. Do you believe that what is best for the team is above everything else (individual or divisional)?

3. Do you believe that our different backgrounds or perspectives should not block our collaboration and our team success?

4. Do you believe that each one of you have something important to contribute, no matter how big or small?

5. Do you believe there are things (even one) that the team should do and we can all agree to?

6. Do you believe that we should set priorities for the steps we should follow?

7. Do you believe that we can agree to a way of prioritizing our tasks (e.g. importance, impact etc.)?

Now you should have reached a good level of consensus. Get ready for the next steps.

1. You need to brainstorm on the things/tasks/strategies the team should follow towards performance and success, or on the problems you should solve.

2. Set a method for prioritization (e.g. through discussion or voting). Make a list in a descending order, starting with things upon which

everyone agrees. Don't forget that the aim is to start with something everyone agrees to, even if this is the smallest one in terms of impact or importance. The goal is to build teamwork, using something they will all be committed and engaged to (since they have reached total consensus).

3. Start implementing the agreed tasks or solutions.

4. Monitor how things are going and take corrective actions.

If you think this is not an easy task, you are absolutely right. It is very difficult to bring together diverse personalities and beliefs, and manage to converge them in order to focus on specific assignments the team needs to deliver. However, you should not forget to acknowledge and **showcase every small success that is accomplished by the team**, showing the positive outcome of their collective effort, hence their successful collaboration. If you manage, through small steps, to make them cooperate and coordinate effectively, you are ready to reach the next level of teamwork, and undertake even bigger and more challenging collaborative steps.

Cultural Embedment

The Synergistic Surplus Model

Acknowledging Diversity

Up till now we have worked on roles and personal characteristics (Knowledge, Skills, Abilities and Other Behavioral Characteristics, KSAOs) that each one brings to the organization or the team, aiming to accomplish common goals under the umbrella of an overall vision. We have identified key strengths and potential hazards, and how you can utilize or overcome them respectively. The core concept of a dynamic management model is diversity and the unique value that individuals contribute to the collective. Now we will more indulge into the concept and find out how **diversity leads to synergy**.

Tapping on diversity requires the development of trust and communication, as well as awareness of the collaborative interdependence (Banks & Millward, 2007). Each one must be accountable and committed to achieving a collective purpose. It requires to openly communicate their unique opinion based on their individual background and perspective. On the other end, they must be willing to accept other people's unique contributions, be supportive, and ready to listen without criticizing (active listening) (Jehn & Bezrukova, 2004; Horwitz, 2005)

Trust and open communication, consistently positive and supportive behaviors, along with clearly defined roles and the respective, right amount of diversity foster the cohesiveness of the team/organization. People are strongly bonded together, and as a discrete live organism (system) are striving to complete their purpose, which is the essence of their existence. **Cohesiveness promotes a team's synergy even more**, since its members care for each other, and are devoted to support each other and develop based on each member's unique contribution to the team.

Synergy occurs when team performance is more than merely the sum of the individual performances (Bowers, et al., 2000; Mohammed & Angell, 2003). But how does this happen? It simply comes up by taking advantage of each member's KSAOs. More specifically, there are things you know and can do, things other people know and can do, and things that you both know and can do. **Convergent KSAOs** enable cooperation. This is the common ground for bringing you together and start communicating by using your shared mental models (Mohammed & Dumville, 2001). It is the "common language" that ignites cooperative conversations. **Divergent KSAOs** are the ones generating the synergistic surplus in KSAOs and eventually performance.

Combining and reconciling each one's exclusive and differentiated knowledge leads **to team learning** (from one another) ending up with a broader perspective, which in turn (and return) results in better ideas and more effective decisions.

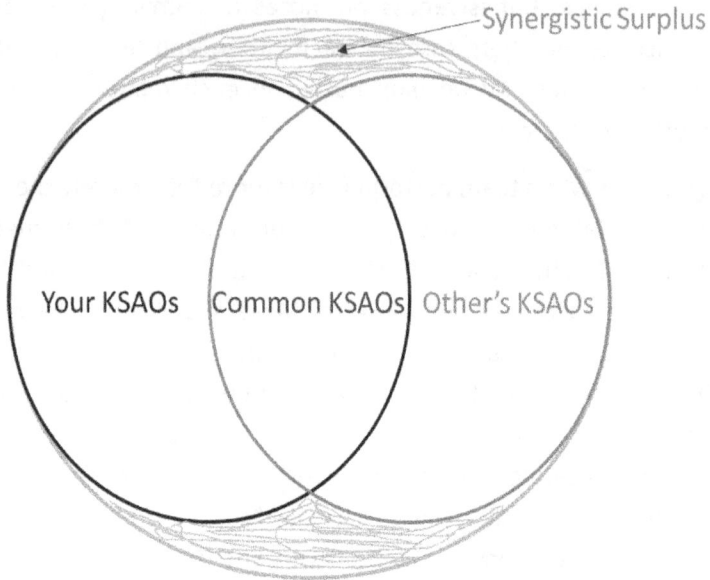

Synergistic Surplus Model
Increasing your Collective Performance

Steps to Synergistic Surplus

Read the following steps and use the tool provided to increase your Synergistic Surplus.

- o Set the context of cooperation (goal, strategy, tactics etc.)

- o Discuss about your common KSAOs

- o Bring up your unique contribution (list what you can add more)

- o Educate one another to each one's exclusive knowledge

- o Plan how you can combine your KSAOs to make it even better (e.g. allocate responsibilities, set communication channels per task, design appropriate decision-making processes, backing up one another's plans)

This should increase your collective performance! The most important thing is to **exchange information as you are working on a project**, as well as helping one another as it goes. Areas of one's weaknesses will be filled by others' strengths. Leadership is most important for synergy, because the leader will foster the appropriate supportive and team-cultured environment that will generate the utilization of unique diversity.

State your collective goal/strategy	
Discuss about your common KSAOs	

Your Unique Contribution	
Name	Contribution

Linking your unique contribution to tasks and roles, and seeing how your cooperation with others (roles/tasks combinations) adds value to the organization or team (see below) may also help you revise your role assignments and the work flow (processes), as designed in previous sections of this book. It may help you be clearer about how you can effectively combine people and roles/tasks.

Link your Unique Contribution to Tasks/Roles				
Member	Task/Role	Communication Channels	Decision Processes	Teammates *(support)*

Storytelling your relationship

Having analyzed your unique contributions and how you can combine them, you may want to further the benefits of synergy and see how it helps to better improve your interpersonal relationships. Use this simple tool, and write a few words of how your cooperation with a person makes a unique contribution to the organization. This should give purpose to your teamwork.

Your name		
Teammate	What are you good at when you come together?	How your cooperation adds value to the organization?

Working Blind Spot

The Collaboration Gap

There is a regular dispute between managers and employees. The former get angry when mistakes happen, think their employees are impotent and lack initiative, and generally they believe they have to make all decisions because they know best (Obolensky, 2007). The latter, in a similar way, believe their managers are incompetent and know nothing about the work, and get frustrated with their leaders' decisions. As you can see from the image below most of the times they are both partially wrong and partially right, because of the existence of a working blind spot.

It is a problem of perspective that hinders effective collaboration. Employees see the whole image of their job issues, but they lose some of the general view of the processes or the work in total. On the other hand, managers see a broader perspective and have different concerns about how the job is processed and connected to a holistic purpose and strategy, but they miss some of the technicalities of the day-to-day tasks. Furthermore both of them miss one another's interests and motivators that affect their decisions and/or actions. The solution is: *instead of accusing, foster a cooperative culture*. **Watch each other's (blind) back**!

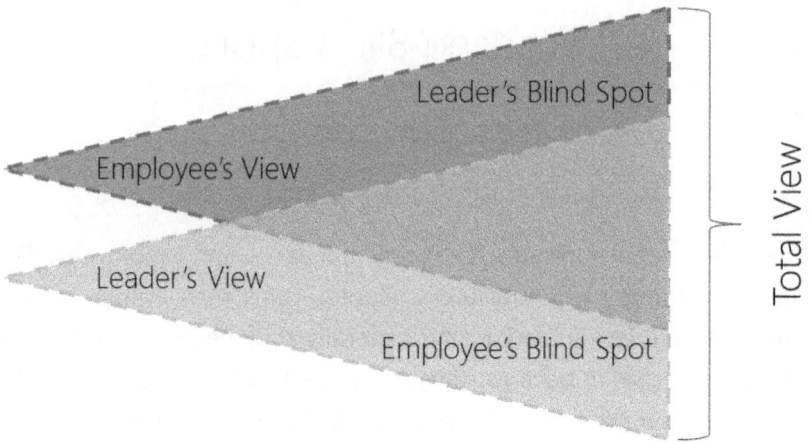

Working Blind Spot Model

The Collaboration Gap

In practice, now, what should you do to overcome this conflict of view? **Open your mind and be receptive to ideas and perspectives**, and if you are the manager/leader, take the first step and pose some questions to yourself and your people.

Ask yourself:

- Do I see the whole picture?

- Is there anything my employees could possibly know better? (list some technical aspects, processes or information/knowledge you probably don't know)

- Am I aware of the problems they encounter delivering their work? (Are you able to list some?)

Ask your people:

- What problems do you encounter? (ask them to list real examples and technicalities)

- How do you think my decisions will impact your work? (ask them to express some realistic predictions)

- What needs to be changed to improve your work? (ask them to list justified suggestions)

- What are the motivators and interests that dictate your decisions/actions

Don't forget to:

- o Explain to your employees the impact that their part of the work has to the rest of the chain.

- o Justify your decisions. They need to be aware of the reasons and the rationale that is probably based on information they don't know.

Information has to flow both ways. Both managers/leaders and employees have to assume that they don't know everything. That is the starting point to go and ask. But, as mentioned, you, as a manager or just a supervisor, need to be the leader and make the first step. However, if you are an employee, don't just wait doing nothing. Take initiative and unlock the information flow by opening your thoughts and asking for more feedback, hoping that you will be truly heard and genuinely understood. Use the tool below to help you close this collaborative gap.

Revealing the Blind Spot (self-awareness)		
Job or Task	List aspects (information, knowledge, processes, technicalities) you probably don't know	List some of the problems your people encounter in their jobs that you are aware of

Unfolding the Blind Spot (taking feedback)			
Job or Task		**Stakeholder**	
What problems do you encounter? *(list real examples and technicalities)*			
How do you think my decisions/actions will impact your work? *(express some realistic predictions)*			
What needs to be changed to improve your work? *(list your justified suggestions)*			
What interests and/or motivators affect your decisions/actions			

Relational Buffering

Sometimes we find it hard to communicate effectively with someone we work with. That person may be a peer, one of our reports, or somebody we report to. **The feeling is stressful**, either anger or frustration or fear, hindering us from sending the appropriate message to the person causing us all these negative feelings. As you can see from the image below the communication with another person is disrupted by negativity. The result is that neither can perform their tasks effectively, holding the working processes and any further development back. If your relationship is impaired, try to **bypass the direct communication path and use someone else as your "Buffer"**. This third person should be someone who has the ability to communicate effectively with both parties and be the intermediate who sends and receives the messages.

Buffer's role is to absorb the negativity and hinder it from passing on to the person on the other end. So, if you are angry with someone and you cannot control your emotions, speak to someone who brings up your better self. Even if your behavior reveals your frustration, it should not have a major effect on the "Buffer" because he/she is not the one the frustration is targeted to. Then the "Buffer" will calmly transmit the appropriate message to the person of interest who in turn will proceed to corrective actions that will positively alter the situation. In a similar way if a person is afraid to speak to you, for whatever the reason, he/she may use the same "Buffer" who has better ability to communicate with you. Then you receive the message and proceed to appropriate actions to respond to the request. Of course this applies vice versa, and with diverse negative feelings and emotions.

However, whatever the problem is, it would be better to try to find a way to resolve your issues and improve your direct relationship and communication. It would not be ideal to use buffering forever. That is why you first need to define the communication problem, then find a person who could temporarily help your working relationship, and in the meantime make the right conversations, and try to reveal the causes and suggest possible solutions. Use the tool below to help you achieve that.

Relational Buffering Tool

You are:		The other is:	
Define the problem			
Who could be the "Buffer" and why?			
Set a discussion plan with the other person			
Causes *(what makes you have negative emotions that hinder you from cooperating effectively)*			
Suggest relational improvement solutions			
Make a solution plan and ask the "Buffer" to input and support			

Learning Organization

In accordance to the dynamic model and the simplistic approach, you have to build a learning organization. **Consider your people and your processes as constantly moving parts of a living system**. I suggested to let your people free to act after you have set the context. It takes time but the only way to succeed is to let them learn from each other as they collaborate and interact, until they find an optimum balance (equilibrium). The model presented below will build your people's receptiveness to behavioral change and constant learning. **Learning capacity unlocks your organization's creativity and ability to change and adapt to the environmental demands** (Dann & Barclay, 2006).

A business is a living organism, which is why it is dynamic, never stable, affecting and affected by its environment. It is an organism consisted of people and as such will also have human weaknesses. Our mind has limited energy capacity, and constantly tries to handle it in an economical manner. That is the reason we act lazy, and we are inherently prone to mistakes (Kahneman, 2011). When we learn something an impression is made in our brain expressed through neural connections which create a certain path. That path is activated whenever we need to retrieve the specific information from our memory (one aspect of knowledge is memory). **Due to energy savings our brain resists to any changes on that path**, hence resisting to creating new knowledge (Strebel, 1996; Houdè, 2013). That is why it is difficult for us to also change our beliefs, and ourselves per se as persons.

The key to an open mind is "Doubt". When we put ourselves in the process of doubting we unfreeze our brain (our neural paths), rendering them susceptible to change. **It takes our focus and energy to do that. It is the difficult way, but it is the way of transformation.** As the model below shows, after unfreezing our brain we are open to new ideas and information, which after collecting them we must examine their validity, through our logic, and if we approve them we learn something new, which again creates a new brain path. The process continues from the beginning. Accept that process for yourself, then cascade it to your people and finally embed it in your learning culture. You will create an organization open to new ideas, and ready to take the risk to try and focus its energy to new things. **That would be a substantial corporate advantage.**

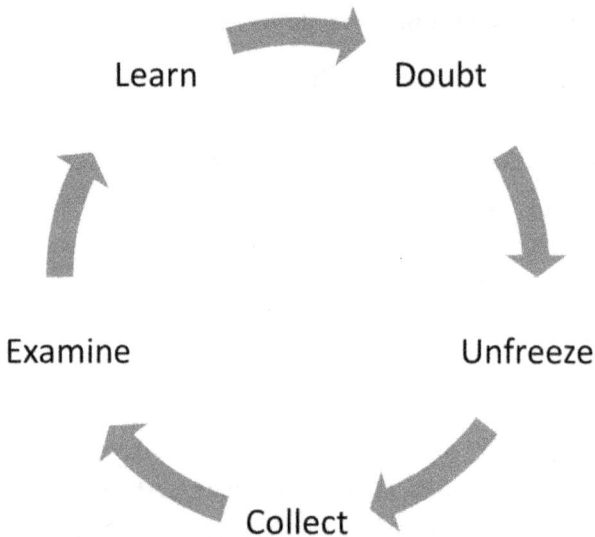

Learn → Doubt

Examine

Unfreeze

Collect

The Circle of Doubt Model

How do you do this? You need to ask questions to yourself and others, just **don't forget to be totally honest with your answers**. Questions would be like:

- Is my belief true (describe your supporting rationale)?

_____

_____

_____

- What could possibly be wrong or negative with my opinion/belief?

_____

_____

_____

- What else could be valid/correct (examine alternatives)?

_____

_____

_____

- What are the positive or correct things about opposite opinions (examine possible benefits)?

_____

_____

_____

L-FET Model

Learning process is your vessel for developing your skills. **When we learn we increase our knowledge capacity, not only in technical but in behavioral skills as well**. Behavioral improvement means that we can be better persons, and *being a better person is a distinct skill on its own*. You realize it when you receive positive behavioral reactions from other people in your everyday interactions, and of course in all kinds of your relationships.

However, ***successful learning has to be deep learning***, which requires total commitment and devotion. Thinking of that I pictured in my mind the L-FET Model for developing your skills. There is no way to be committed in learning new skills, if you are not internally motivated. That's what the "L" stands for. **You have to do something you Love doing**. Your love will provide you with the sufficient amount of focus you have to put on your effort. That's the "F" of the model. But as nothing comes without energy cost in the part of our brain, focus is what drives your energy to the selected area of learning for an effective self-development process. Obviously, energy is you "E" in the learning model.

We still have to define the "T" part of the model, and this is **the gift of Time**. You may love doing something, you may decide to dedicate your focus and energy at the expense of other activities, but in order to do all of these you need to also dedicate your time, also at the expense of other activities in your professional and personal life. Saving time also contributes to the amount of energy we invest in our self-development. As the image below shows, love is the internal motivator that pushes skill development forward, and the initial step. Then, when focus is secured we are halfway there to find the amount of energy we need. The other half will come from time-saving, which means that we pull time from other activities. Hence, time is the external denominator which is also affected by other factors than ourselves.

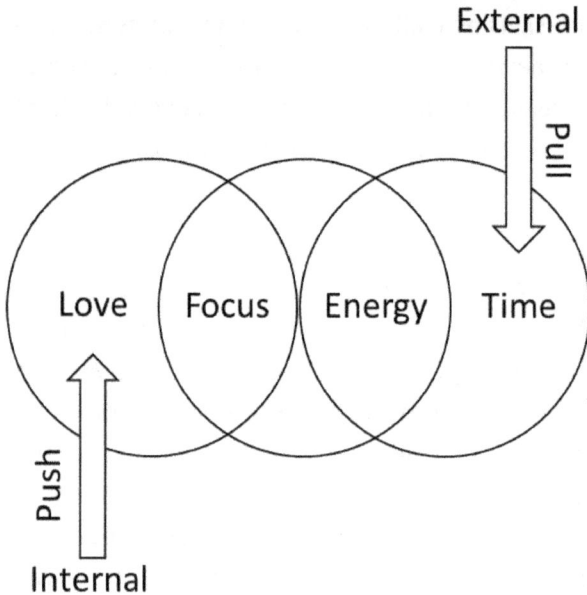

L-FET Model

This is the big bet, how to secure your time for doing things you love when everybody in your life asks for your time, whether this is your boss, your family, your clients etc. So, **the question is who will give you the gift of time**, the most valuable external resource for your own development. I would say probably no one will provide you with that present, just because everybody asks for something, a piece of your time. My suggestion is that **you have to claim that gift for yourself**. Create your own time slots, and demand not to be disturbed. Choose the "when", ask everyone to respect it, and then undisrupted drive your focus and your energy to your learning goals.

I understand we live in a hectic and complex world, and that we cannot ignore people's requests when they ask or need something from us. We are social beings and we need each other's support. However, I believe we can find a relational time balance and secure our own time. It doesn't have to be long, it could even be 3-4 hours during the weekend. But during that time, our own time, we have to be totally engaged. And **as focus is necessary for concentrating our energy, target one skill at a time**. Energy is scarce and if divided in smaller pieces, our effectiveness drops in all aspects.

Defining Knowledge

Speaking of knowledge we have to clarify its concept. **Knowledge is memory and data combination**. When we say we know things we actually mean we remember things, but knowledge is not only what we know (remember), but what we do with it. Knowledge counts for nothing unless we use it to make our decisions, and the more information we have the more probable it is to make a correct decision (Kahneman, 2011). But as information increases in amount the more we feel the need to combine it in a proper (correct and effective) way, and this is a skill we need to develop.

We have to accept though the fact that **knowledge comes with awareness and desperation**. As we climb the mountain of knowledge, in the beginning we learn a great deal of things regarding a specific subject or discipline. And we feel great, even arrogant sometimes, looking down on others who know nothing or less about it.

However, as we climb towards higher levels of knowledge and get more experts on the area, the amount of things we learn gets narrower because adding knowledge gets harder as we go up. We have to collect its parts piece by piece, once we want to indulge into it. And then we conquer the peak of the mountain, and desperation comes. Our horizon has been expanded and we just realize that we have mastered only one dot in the universe of knowledge.

The frustration notwithstanding, **when we conquer a top is when we become real learners**, with modesty and respect. We are aware that even though we know a lot, we know nothing comparing to the total knowledge, and that makes us try to learn more. We open our minds, we doubt even our own opinions and beliefs, we think creatively, and consequently we seek new learning adventures. This is when the circle of doubt, presented previously, really starts to work.

Decision Making

There are numerous theories and techniques for advancing your decision making in many aspects of your professional and personal life. Making a decision always has a risk. Most of the times we sacrifice something to gain something else. Everything comes with a cost. Before making a decision, we need to think not only about the alternative options but the alternative outcomes that each option comes with. Then we should ask ourselves: "**Can I bare it**"?

I will now give my approach to decision making, which has helped me a lot during my life. As I noted just before, the main query is whether I can stand the cost that comes with every decision, and if I can live with the possible negative consequences. So, **I think, and I think well before I act**. Decision making needs time, so we can overcome our inherent tendency to make fast intuitive decisions (Kandel, 2008; Kahneman, 2011). Time gives space to our logic to take over and analyze all the available information.

I follow a simple three-step technique to make the best decision I can, given the circumstances: **I simplify the concept/situation, I project it to the future, and I take it to its extremes**.

1. **Simplifying a concept or situation**: when you are thinking of a situation or a concept, you need to understand it first. Most of the times they are complicated so we need to break them down to their fundamental dimensions, before we can clearly see what they mean and how they work.

2. **Projecting into the future**: projection gives you the opportunity to visualize the possible outcomes that will come in the future after you act upon your decisions.

3. **Taking it to its extremes**: it's another way to better understand how a concept or a phenomenon works and what you will have to deal with in terms of negative or positive consequences. It's like testing the situation and yourself.

You may utilize each step separately or in combination, depending on the situation and what would work best. However, whatever you do, no matter how you make your decisions, **you need to be honest with yourself**, do not be ashamed of your own thoughts. **Thoughts are not desires, and desires are not actions.** So, think freely and from multiple perspectives without criticizing your own thoughts.

Finally, it's ok to use numbers and formulas to make your decisions, but remember that numbers do tell the truth we have set them to tell. Hence, they are susceptible to human mistakes, they can be wrong if the parameters we set are also wrong. Let numbers aid you but do not fully depend on them.

"Thoughts are not desires, and desires are not actions"

Antonis Gavalas

Learning from Mistakes Model

An important aspect of a learning culture is for a business to learn from its own mistakes. As we said before, an organization incorporates all the shortfalls an individual human encounters. **We are mistake-prone by design** (Klein, 2007; Lucht & Rosskopf, 2008; Homsma, et al., 2009). Mistakes may come from our inexperience or from our over-confidence. As our experience increases the probabilities of us making mistakes significantly decrease but never fully disappear. Since there is always a chance, even a small one, for mistakes to occur, and since **we don't know the time of their occurrence**, our brain vigilance is a prerequisite at all the times.

Since we agree that mistakes happen and we cannot avoid them, the issue raised here is what we do with them. **We just love them, as we love ourselves, because they are part of our own existence!** When we accept them without guilt, we let them drive us towards our learning and improvement. When I say 'to love them' I do not imply to be after them. We must avoid them proactively, but in case they occur we need to take the best they can give us: **a lesson**.

My model of how we can learn from mistakes consists of *three motivational stages towards learning*. *Remember that perfection is the drive, not the result.* Hereafter I present my model based on our inherent tendency to make mistakes.

Stage 1 – *Prediction*: awareness of our tendency to make mistakes increases our focus. We are vigilant and we plan contingency plans in case they eventually occur. That process of trying to avoid our mistakes leads us to learning, through observation, and gathering new information and knowledge, and by combining our own and other people's experiences. In that way we get better and also decrease probabilities of mistakes.

Stage 2 – _Avoidance_: we don't like mistakes, we encounter them as a threat, and as such mistake avoidance also increases our focus and energy, making an effort to improve ourselves and do our job better. Willingness to avoid mistakes is an important incentive for us to utilize and improve our knowledge in order not to make them.

Stage 3 – _Learning_: as we said we eventually do not avoid making a mistake. This is the stage of learning from an actually occurred mistake. We need to stay calm, and offer a solution which is translated as new knowledge, a new experience, which in turn helps us refrain ourselves from making the same mistake again in the future.

The model appears in a circle depicting its perpetually continuous process. It has neither a beginning nor an end, it is a vicious circle which leads to ever-going learning. Mistakes are a reliable source of learning because as threats they are ringing a bell in our minds telling us that we should take action. We need to change our neural structure and learn new things. But it is a non-stop process because, as we know from neuroscience, one aspect of knowledge is memory and memory deteriorates through time and inactivity (Kandel et al., 2011). So we must constantly keep focused and acute.

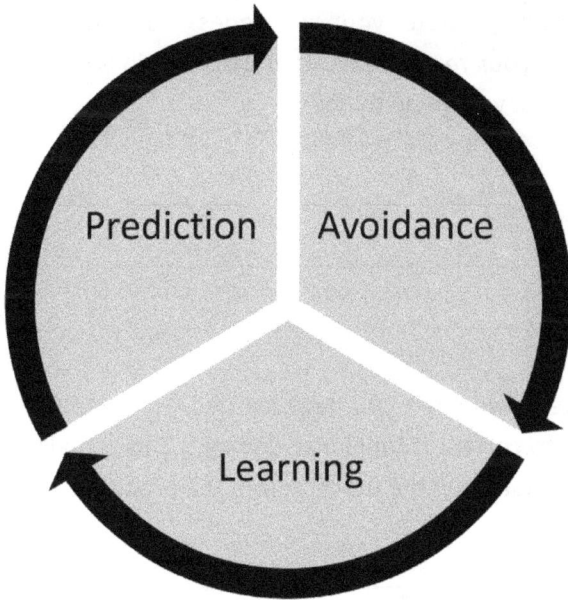

Learning from Mistakes Model

Translating the model's stages into an action plan, you should follow the three steps below:

Prepare: ask yourself and others what could possibly go wrong and what actions you should take to avoid them.

_____

_____

_____

Commit yourself: state your willingness to avoid mistakes and acknowledge your responsibilities and actions in your effort to avoid them (what are you going to do?).

_____

_____

_____

Learn: write down what you have learned from a mistake and what you will do to correct it (minimize damage) and actually prepare not to do it again (starting the process from the preparation step).

_____

_____

_____

Leading by Mistakes

What does that model has to offer to leadership? Management at all levels must recognize and accept the fact that mistakes happen and that we need to **generate a mistake-tolerant culture** (Homsma, et al., 2009). Making mistakes is not to be punished, unless it is due to indifference and unprofessionalism. In that case, I don't think you need those kind of people in your team/organization. An organization has to sustain a consistently rewarding system. You cannot reward your people one day and punish them the next, otherwise rewarding will have no meaning to them and it will not motivate them. People need not to be afraid, they need to be open to learning from their failures. Management should then stand by them and help them improve themselves by changing the context, and training them for new skills, and behaviors (Catino & Patriotta, 2013).

I don't imply that the message should be "feel free to make mistakes", but rather **"feel safe to make mistakes"**. That motto leads them to the learning from mistakes model, and they should be indulged in that. That means they must plan to avoid mistakes, they should be focused and committed trying not to actually make them, and if they eventually happen to learn from them in order for them not to reoccur in the future.

It is a human characteristic, a part of our life, but a paradox happens: **humanity progresses through a battery of failures and mistakes**. It seems like we cannot advance without them. Organizations are not different. They are part of our society and life cycle, and need to be managed according to our natural traits, i.e. abilities and weaknesses.

You can do much to help your people avoid mistakes. Technology and psychology have offered many tools and techniques to that direction. You can set standardized procedures that minimize probabilities of mistakes. Discuss with your team about the risks, and decide how you can predict and avoid.

Some steps found in literature that may help are the following (e.g. David, 2001; Dale, 2003):

1. Map your work

2. Locate probable risks

3. Brainstorm on how you can avoid them

4. Set accountability of selected actions

5. Predict disasters and predetermine your reactions to minimize losses.

Remember that experience minimizes risks but does not eradicate them. You should constantly be vigilant, calm, and open-minded. Help one another by creating a mistake-tolerant and supportive organizational culture.

"You never know how and when you affect someone's life with something you say or do, no matter how big or small, simple or complex. Consistency is all that matters.

Be a role model at all times!"

Antonis Gavalas

Kill the General

Stay Calm

Your role as supervisor, manager or top leader is to **stand before threats and disruptiveness with courage, patience, and a clear mind**. Remember that you have the responsibility of other people, and you have to be their role model should you want them to also deal with difficulties. Then, as a cohesive team you will find the solution to every problem, to every mistake or unpredicted situation.

How do you think they will feel if they see you under a panic attack every time something bad happens? They will feel they cannot depend on your support during a disruptive occurrence nor will they believe you can lead them out of it and back into serenity. Even worse, when they make a mistake, they will try to hide it instead of bringing it out for a solution to be found. They will act like children fearing of you scorning them every time they are being mischievous. That is not right! Such behaviors do not build trust.

Think that you are the general and they are the soldiers during a fatal combat. Would they trust you if you get easily upset, angry, afraid, or stressed? You make the significant final decisions, their life is in your hands. Would they depend on you? Probably not. They will not be able to fight as long as you are on the lead, and the battle will be lost. The only thing in their minds will be to either get you out of the way or they will lose the battle and probably their lives. The only solution from their perspective is to "kill the general" (not literally of course, probably relieve him of his duties). That is what would happen in a combat field. **In the business world they will just try to leave and go out on a search for another battle (job challenge).**

High Performing Organization

If you read literature, and if you combine it with your own experiences, you will find numerous factors determining and/or affecting team or organizational performance (Barry & Stewart, 1997; Bell, 2007). However, as already presented above, I suggest that three dimensions are the essence of performance: **Roles, Communication,** and **Trust.** The rationale is that performance means teamwork. A team or organization consists of people with diverse backgrounds, hence at the very core of performance lies the ability to coordinate and collaborate efficiently and effectively (Rico, et al., 2008). To do that you need to set and assign clear responsibilities and decision-making authority, so everyone knows what, how, when, and why they are doing it. Then roles are combined into a solid process system, and people need to develop their interpersonal relationships to coordinate effectively. For that they need to trust each other and develop their communication skills, and establish appropriate communication channels. If these three dimensions are in place you will have created the base for further improving performance by adding more motivational factors, and promoting more innovative working and management systems which would engage your people even more.

These three dimensions generate the **Least Required Performance Index** for reaching high levels of performance. They indicate your organization is well-functioning, and your people know what and how to contribute to it. If one of them is missing, your performance will be disrupted. Their importance is depicted graphically by the "**Upside-Down Performance Triangle**". Trust is the most important factor to overcome any obstacles, and work towards team results and performance. It lies at the reversed upper peak of the triangle indicating that performance is balancing over trust, and the slightest inclination would tear everything down. Roles are the base of performance dictating organizational functionality, and communication lies in the middle, binding the processes (and dimensions). Communication is actually the behavioral expression of the other two dimensions.

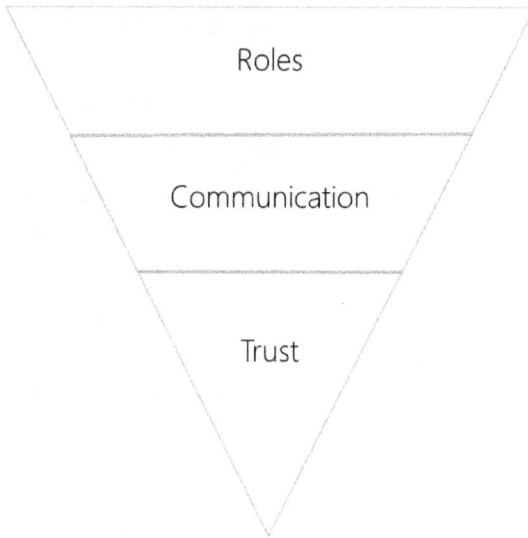

Upside-Down Performance Triangle

Assessing your Least Required Performance Index

Rate your performance in each of the following statements of the three dimensions (RCT), from 1 (totally disagree) to 10 (totally agree), and then add your scores. Each member of your team or organization should answer the questionnaire. You should then calculate the average of your subtotals.

Roles

1) Each one knows what to do and how to contribute to team/organization.

2) We never let each other down as far as our responsibilities are concerned.

3) We deliver what is expected from us and in time.

4) We know from whom and when to ask for help if necessary.

5) We are aware of each other's roles and responsibilities, expectations and obligations, needs and difficulties.

6) Our cooperation and coordination are efficient and effective.

7) Process flow is clear, well-structured and smooth.

8) We know whom to cooperate and coordinate with to fulfil our role.

9) We know who's reporting to whom.

10) We have enough authority and freedom to make decisions to complete our tasks.

Communication

1) We understand and use the formal and informal communication channels, keeping regular contact with colleagues.

2) We carefully and sincerely listen without judging or jumping into conclusions. We patiently wait to take our turn to speak.

3) There is consistency in our messages, verbal or non-verbal.

4) We value social conversations.

5) Communication channels are clear and well-structured. We are all aware of whom we should communicate with to do our job.

6) We respect and consider each other's opinion. We don't try to impose our own.

7) When we communicate we confirm that the message has been received and understood.

8) We are aware of and consider each other's emotions.

Trust

1) We support each other in personal and work-related matters.

2) We are open and honest.

3) We respect each other's unique personality, value and emotions.

4) There is consistency in our words and actions.

5) We exchange important information without fear.

6) We depend on each other's support to complete our task.

7) We are discrete.

8) We are not afraid of investing in long-term relationships.

9) We don't accuse or try to find someone to blame.

10) There is a good environment of cooperation within our team/organization.

Score

High	201-280	Your team functions very well, but you should take actions in order to sustain and/or further develop your performance.
Average	141-200	Your performance is satisfactory, but you have many things to do and work hard for further development.
Low	28-140	You probably encounter disruptive problems within your team/organization. You should consider redesigning your processes and promote behavioral development.

Note: *These assessments may also be conducted separately, if you wish to measure a specific dimension. In that case the score interpretation should be adapted accordingly. For example, measuring only Trust, low score will be from 10 to 50, average score will be from 51 to 70, and high score from 71 to 100.*

Please mind that this assessment tool is not standardized and it should be used as an isolate index of your performance. If you want to retest yourself or your team to measure your progress through time, as a rule of thumb, only a difference of 7 points and above (plus or minus) should be considered as a significant change.

Now that you have rated your performance index try to detect those areas that are most problematic. Locate the areas that you had low scores, turn them into negative statements or questions and try to find improvement solutions. For example, if you scored low on "We depend on each other's support to complete our task", make it "We cannot depend on each other's support to complete our task" or "Why can we not depend on each other's support to complete our task?"

Area of improvement	What actions should we take to improve?	Stakeholders	Time & Resources

Remedy

There is an inherent variability in every living system in nature. That makes them unpredictable and prone to disruption. The universe is not only encoded to create life but destruction as well. We may hypothesize that life cannot exist without destruction, in fact that life is born through death.

Consequently, there is always a chance that something goes wrong. In that case we need to intervene and correct any inefficiencies. So, each system built by us should come with its own remedy plan. Sometimes, problems are well hidden, and we cannot even see them causing harm to our collective performance. Tactical monitoring is required.

But this process should also be used for detecting opportunities, based on the continuous change and improvement approach. Opportunities should be in alignment with the environmental needs. Follow the steps below and openly communicate any problems or opportunities for further team/organizational development.

1. Frequently meet to discuss problems and opportunities for improvement.

2. Write down your processes, and analyze them step by step.

3. Detect technical and/or behavioral problems

4. Detect development opportunities (without necessarily pertaining to any problems)

5. Generate solutions and/or suggestions

6. Plan their implementation

7. Monitor their progress

It is a non-stop process that should be followed by all stakeholders. Correcting any inefficiencies will increase performance and profitability, and also improve interpersonal relationships, since process interactions will be flowing without interruptions. The younger the system, the more its possible disruptions. However, as previously noted, failures and mistakes are never totally eradicated. A "garden" needs constant caring to look tidy and beautiful. In the same way our business needs continuous support to keep running smoothly, and effectively.

Don't forget though that we are fostering a liberal system which will find its own equilibrium. Tasks' stakeholders should be the ones suggesting solutions and improvements since they will also be responsible for implementing any decisions made. You don't have to impose, just propose and support. They know their work and they will find the way to make their life easier and more productive.

Protect your People

There are too many adversities that your people encounter in their everyday job activities. Those difficulties emanate from internal factors such as technical problems, process flaws and interpersonal relationships, as well as from external factors such as clients, suppliers, and other stakeholders relationships. They need your support to overcome them!

What usually happens is that they also have to deal with a disrupting relationship with you, the supervisor or the business owner. That affects their commitment to your organizations' values and strategy. You tend to believe that your people work for you because they believe in you, but most of the times this is a misperception. They work for you because you pay them.

The reason they don't believe in organizational values, and don't love to work for you is because you do not protect them from harm, wherever that comes from. You just see them as value-creating units, not as humans, and in return they see you as an "ATM", just having to press some buttons, to do their task and get the money.

What you have to do is to LISTEN to their thoughts. Listen to their problems, and do it every day. They will appreciate it. And then do something about it. They will really believe in you. They will work for your organization because they will love working for someone who cares. And if someday they leave, don't consider them ungrateful. They just want to test their strengths to chase their dreams, to challenge their opportunities. But they will always have to say some good words about you and your organization. **They will be your advertisers**.

> ### *Here's a real case scenario*
>
> There was a travel agency employee who had had provided group boat tickets to a regular customer. The customer wanted to cancel the tickets, and the employee informed him that it was too late for cancelation, and that cancelation fees applied. That was the normal process, the rules set by the shipping company. However, just because he was a regular customer, the employee also said to him that he would ask his employer if there was anything they could do about it. Then the customer start yelling, saying that he would find another agency office to cooperate with.
>
> The employee remained calm, wondering if this was his fault, and if he should have handled the situation differently, i.e. cancel the tickets without the penalty. But, this was something beyond his authority to decide. When the employer came back to the office, the employee informed her about the incident. Her reaction was "That is what he said! Ok, don't worry, I'll handle it". She then called the customer and made it clear that he had no right to yell at her employee for doing his job, and that if he wished to find another supplier he was welcome to do so.

That was a small example of protecting your people. Difficulties are coming from everywhere. Your people just need to feel safe, that you are a cohesive team supporting one another against adversities. Of course that takes mutual respect and understanding of what each member is dealing with in their role. It also implies that each one is appropriately doing his/her job according to the organization's values and strategy. Just remember that mistakes happen and they are a good source of learning and improvement, they are not meant to be punished. Indifference is the disruptive behavior that should be discouraged.

Don't act like a star, act like a mate, like a wingman. Think and ask yourself: **do you want around you people who will be ready to sacrifice themselves for you or people who stay just because you pay them?** The latter will never respect you nor support you (forever). They will be next to you as long as they need you. After that, they will leave.

Epilogos

The Garden Effect Model is a dynamic management approach which enables people to freely act and interact, and adapt or change by reading the environmental trends and factors, and by learning on the process from each other. It is a process that begins by clarifying the context, and progressively liberates people as they gain experience on the job and on their interpersonal relationships (how they interact together).

How much freedom should we delegate? As much as the specific organization or situation (or we) can take. In theory you can leave the system totally uninspected after you have set the vision and the social (and ethical) purpose of the organization or the team. **The system will find the way to thrive by utilizing its own knowledge and interacting dynamics**. It will perform and continuously improve. Think of that system as a spinning top. You set direction and momentum and then it spins on its own. If you then try to interfere, you will only disturb the system and it will probably fall down. Your role is to provide your support when the system loses its direction or its momentum.

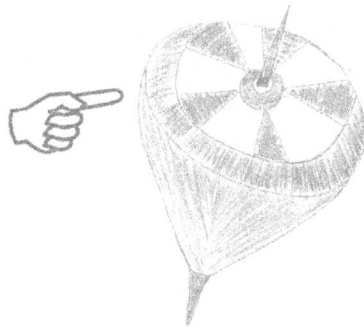

Think of your organization as a system, like societies, like the universe itself, and follow the example of nature which always finds its way to life. Energy and space are scarce and finite. There is a constant fight between the components of a system. Follow the universal harmony that leads to perpetuity, and not to destruction. That is **the effect of the right balance between collective equilibrium and individual freedom**. We have adopted so much knowledge from nature that helped us progress. Think of the sonar system, our capability to fly, and many more. Why not let nature do the work? **Let the system do what it knows best – live**. Your role is to watch the inherent inefficiencies that lead to deterioration and destruction, and if need be, reset the context, give the momentum back.

I also suggest that you watch how sport teams operate within the time frame of a single game. There is much preparation behind the scenes, but you can see so many team characteristics applying in a short period of time. **Observe the high performing teams and you will see that a balance between a well-structured context and freedom of decisions (in a matter of seconds) discriminate the successful ones**. The coach is just watching if what they have set is working and if not he/she gives new directions.

Sustaining Engagement - An Equilibrium System

Engagement is a reciprocal and dynamic dependent system. On the one hand, an organization must provide the right context and on the other hand individuals must have the willingness to perform, where the latter stands as an inner motivational factor and energy devotion. That level of engagement asks for a system which is fair and equal, otherwise the system itself will fall apart, and its dynamics will be disconnected and disoriented.

The same policies and environmental factors may have different effects on different people, just because people have different needs, perspectives, and behaviors. Everything is depending on the system, and a dynamic system as the one I propose also takes individuality under consideration, in that every employee gets to be satisfied. **A liberal working system will reach collective performance through appropriately recognizing our human individuality.** People need to have all the necessary space to "move", adapt, and develop by adjusting their aspirations, interests and abilities (strengths) to the organizational needs. In that way everyone is happy. Individuals accomplish their own development and the team or organization reaches high levels of effectiveness and performance, according to market needs and demands. It is a win-win situation.

As a reminder, keep that it is not easy. **It is easier giving orders than delegating actual freedom.** Freedom comes with great responsibility for the one who is granting it and for the one who takes it. You have to patiently build it through time. People need time to absorb something new and accept it before transforming through their development. Don't get misled by those who propose quick techniques to personal or team transformation. **The caterpillar will not transform into a butterfly unless it puts itself in a cocoon.** You first have to retreat, and then devote time, focus, and energy.

Theorists and practitioners of leadership usually talk about the complex and disruptive world we live in. They mostly suggest ways to bail us out from this situation, when the solution is to stop perpetuating disruptiveness.

"We fear our own creation. We struggle to deal with a complex world that we create."

Antonis Gavalas

Index

K

KSAOs, 6, 9, 10, 16, 59, 67, 106, 107, 108, 110

L

leadership, 2, 3, 4, 5, 7, 14, 16, 19, 26, 64, 68, 78, 79, 82, 83, 84, 85, 86, 87, 137

learning, 3, 5, 14, 16, 19, 20, 21, 26, 30, 38, 64, 68, 74, 94, 95, 107, 121, 122, 125, 127, 129, 133, 134, 137, 151, 153

M

mature, 22, 82, 83

maturity, 5, 16, 20, 21, 25, 83

motivation, 3, 5, 21, 40, 46, 67, 99, 103

motivational, 26, 133, 141, 154

O

organizational context, 20, 87

P

performance, 1, 4, 5, 11, 15, 18, 19, 26, 31, 34, 40, 44, 47, 48, 56, 58, 61, 67, 68, 84, 86, 95, 104, 107,

109, 141, 142, 146, 147, 148, 149, 155

personal development, 46, 64, 84, 99

processes, 1, 11, 16, 17, 20, 22, 25, 26, 27, 30, 32, 34, 35, 44, 52, 57, 61, 63, 67, 84, 85, 94, 98, 109, 111, 113, 114, 116, 118, 121, 142, 146, 148

R

relational, 22, 37, 45, 48, 52, 56, 92, 120, 127

relationships, 1, 4, 26, 31, 34, 38, 40, 45, 47, 48, 52, 56, 61, 69, 71, 81, 82, 84, 85, 89, 112, 125, 141, 145, 149, 150, 153

responsibility, 4, 7, 18, 21, 46, 84, 92, 99, 140, 155

roles, 1, 3, 6, 10, 16, 22, 26, 31, 32, 34, 35, 47, 48, 56, 61, 63, 67, 69, 71, 72, 74, 76, 106, 111, 141, 143

S

simplicity, 18, 19, 23, 25, 29, 31, 67, 74, 80, 82

supportiveness, 5, 38, 89

T

Trust, 4, 5, 89, 102, 103, 106, 141, 145, 146

References

Alper, S., Tjosvold, D. and Law, K.S., 1998, Interdependence and Controversy in Group Decision Making: Antecedents to Effective Self-Managing Teams, Organizational Behavior and Human Decision Processes, Vol. 74, No 1, pp. 33-52

Bailey, J., 2007, "Profile lateral thinking: Edward De Bono", *Engineering Management Journal*, Vol. 17, No 5, pp. 46-47

Banks, A.P., Millward, L.J., 2007, "Differentiating Knowledge in Teams: The Effect of Shared Declarative and Procedural Knowledge on Team Performance", Group Dynamics: Theory, Research, and Practice, Vol. 11, No 2, pp 95-106

Barrick, M.R., Mount, M.K., 1991, "The Big Five Personality Dimensions and Job Performance: A Meta-Analysis", Personnel Psychology, Vol. 44, pp 1-26

Barrick, M.R., Stewart, L.G., Neubert, M.J., Mount, M.K., 1998, "Relating Member Ability and Personality to Work-Team Processes and Team Effectiveness", Journal of Applied Psychology, Vol. 83, No 3, pp 377-391

Barry, B., Stewart, G.L., 1997, "Composition, Process, and Performance in Self-Managed Groups: The Role of Personality", Journal of Applied Psychology, Vol. 82, No 1, pp 62-78

Bell, S.T., 2007, "Deep-Level Composition Variables as Predictors of Team Performance: A Meta-Analysis", Journal of Applied Psychology, Vol. 92, No 3, pp 595-615

Borman, W.C., Penner, L.A., Allen, T.D., Motowidlo, S.J., 2001, "Personality Predictors of Citizenship Performance", International Journal of Selection and Assessment, Vol. 9, No 1&2, pp 52-69

Boulton, J. and Allen, P., 2007. Complexity and strategy. In: Jenkins, M., Ambrosini, V. and Collier, N., eds. Advanced Strategic Management: A Multi-Perspective Approach. Basingstoke: Palgrave Macmillan.

Bowers, C.A., Pharmer, J.A., Salas, E., 2000, "When Member Homogeneity is Needed in Work Teams: A Meta-Analysis", Small Group Research, Vol. 31, No 3, pp 305-327

Caldwell, B.S., Everhart, N.C., 1998, "Information flow and Development of Coordination in Distributed supervisory Control Teams", International Journal of Human-Computer Interaction, Vol. 10, No 1, pp 51-70

Caldwell, B.S., 2005, "Multi-Team dynamics and Distributed Expertise in Mission Operations", Aviation, Space, and Environmental Medicine, Vol. 76. No 6, pp 145-153

Callaway, M.R., Marriott, R.G., Esser, J.K., 1985, "Effects of Dominance on Group Decision Making: Toward a Stress-Reduction Explanation of Groupthink", Journal of Personality and Social Psychology, Vol. 49, No 4, pp 949-952

Catino, M., Patriotta, G., 2013, "Learning from Errors: Cognition, Emotions and Safety Culture in the Italian Air Force", Organization Studies, Vol. 34, No. 4, pp. 437-467

Cohen, S.G., Bailey, D.E., 1997, "What Makes Teams Work: Group Effectiveness Research from the Shop Floor to the Executive Suite", Journal of Management, Vol. 23, No 3, pp 239-290

Cookson, L.J., 2013, "A Desire for Parsimony", Behavioral Sciences, Vol. 3, pp. 576-586

Dale, B.G., 2003, Managing Quality, fourth edition, Blackwell, Oxford

Dann, Z. and Barclay, I. (2006) "Complexity Theory and Knowledge Management Application", The Electronic Journal of Knowledge Management, Volume 4 Issue 1, pp 11-20, available online at www.ejkm.com

David R.F., 2001, Strategic Management concepts & cases, eighth edition, Prentice Hall

De Bono, E., 1992, Serious creativity: Using the power of lateral thinking to create new ideas, New York, NY: HarperCollins Publishers, Inc.

Eisenhardt, K. and H. Piezunka, 2011, "Complexity and corporate strategy", Sage Handbook of Complexity and Management. P. Allen, S. Maguire and B. McKelvey. 506-523

Epstein, R., 1984, "The Principle of Parsimony and Some Applications in Psychology", *The Journal of Mind and Behavior*, Volume 5, No. 2, pp. 119-130

Flin, R., O'Connor, P., Mearns, K., 2002, "Crew resource management: improving team work in high reliability industries", Team Performance Management: An International Journal, Vol. 8, No 3/4, pp 68-78

Frese, M., Gielnik, MM., 2014, "The Psychology of Entrepreneurship", *The Annual Review of Organizational Psychology and Organizational Behavior*, Vol. 1, pp. 413-438

Gittell, J.H., 2002, "Coordinating Mechanisms in Care Provider Groups: Relational Coordinations a Mediator and Input Uncertainty as a Moderator of Performance Effects", Management Science, Vol. 48, No 11, pp 1408-1426

Harrison, D.A., Price, K.H., Gavin, J.H., Florey, A.T., 2002, "Time, Teams, and Task Performance: Changing Effects of Surface- and Deep-Level Diversity on Group Functioning", Academy of Management Journal, Vol. 45, No 5, pp 1029-1045

Helmreich, R.L., Merrit, A.C., 2000, Safety and error management: The role of Crew Resource Management. In B.J. Hayward & A.R. Lowe (Eds.), Aviation Resource Management (pp. 107-119). Aldershot, UK: Ashgate

Hogan, J., Holland, B, 2003, "Using Theory to Evaluate Personality and Job-Performance Relations: A Socioanalytic Perspective", Journal of Applied Psychology, Vol. 88, No 1, pp 100-112

Homsma, G.J., Van Dyck, C., De Gilber, D., Koopman, P.L., Elfring, T., 2009, "Learning from error: The influence of error incident characteristics", Journal of Business Research, Vol. 62, pp. 115-122

Horwitz, S.K., 2005, "The Compositional Impact of Team Diversity on Performance: Theoretical Considerations", Human Resource Development Review, Vol. 4, No 2, pp 219-245

Houdè, Olivier, 2013, The *Psychology of a Child*, Vesta Editions, Thessaloniki

Jehn, K.A., Bezrukova, K., 2004, "A field study of group diversity, workgroup context, and performance", Journal of Organizational Behavior, Vol. 25, pp 703-729

Kahneman, D., 2011, *Thinking Fast and Slow*, Penguin Books, Great Britain

Kandel, E.,R., et al, 2011, *Neuroscience and Behaviour*, University Editions of Crete, Heraklion

Kandel, R.Eric., 2008, In Search of Memory: the emergence of a new science of mind, University Editions of Crete, Heraklion

Kantas, A., 1995, *Organisational – Industrial Psychology*, Vol. 3, Ellinika Grammata, Athens

Kiffin-Petersen, A.S., Cordery, L.J., 2003, "Trust, individualism and mob characteristics as predictors of employee preference for teamwork", The International Journal of Human Resource Management, Vol. 14, No 1, pp 93-116

Klein, T.A., Neumann, J., Reuter, M., Hennig, J., von Cramon, D.Y., Ullsperger, M., 2007, "Genetically Determined Differences in Learning from Errors", Science, Vol. 318, pp. 1642-45

Kliegel, M., Jager, T., 2006, "The Influence of Negative Emotions on Prospective Memory: A Review an New Data (Invited Paper)", *International Journal of Computational Cognition*, Vol. 4, No. 1, pp. 1-17

Kouzes, J.M., Posner, B.Z., 2003, *The Leadership Challenge,* 3rd edition, Jossey-Bass, USA

Lucht, M., Rosskopf, D., 2008, "Comment on Genetically Determined differences in Learning from Errors", Science, Vol. 321, p. 200a

Markey, P.M., Funder, D.C., Ozer, D.J., 2003, "Complementarity of Interpersonal Behaviors in Dyadic Interactions", *The Society for Personality and Social Psychology*, Vol. 29, No 9, pp 1082-1090

Mathieu, E.J., Heffner, S.T., Goodwin, F.G., Salas, E., Cannon-Bowers, A.J., 2000, "The Influence of Shared Mental Models on Team Process and Performance", Journal of Applied Psychology, Vol. 85, No 2, pp 273-283

McDonald, J.M., Keys, J.B., 1996, "The seven deadly sins of teambuilding", Team Performance Management, Vol. 2, No 2, pp 19-26

McElroy, W., M., 2000, "Integrating complexity theory, knowledge management and organizational learning", *Journal of Knowledge Management*, Vol. 4 . No. 3, pp. 195-203

Mohammed, S., Angell, L.C., 2003, "Personality Heterogeneity in Teams: Which Differences Make a Difference for Team Performance?", Small Group Research, Vol. 34, No 6

Mohammed, S., Dumville, B.C., 2001, "Team mental models in a team knowledge framework: expanding theory and measurement across disciplinary boundaries", Journal of Organizational Behavior", Vol. 22, pp 89-106

Montuori, Alfonso. "General Systems Theory." International Encyclopedia of Organization Studies. 2007. SAGE Publications. 1 Mar. 2009. <http://sage-reference.com/organization/Article_n192.html>.

Nullmeyer, R.T., Spiker, V.A., 2003, "The Importance of Crew Resource Management Behaviors in Mission Performance: Implications for Training Evaluation", Military Psychology, Vol. 15, No 1, pp 77-96

Obolensky, N., 2007, *Chaos Leadership and Polyarchy – countering leadership stress?*, Extended Essay Series, Centre for Leadership Studies, University of Exeter

Partington, D., Harris, H., 1999, "Team role balance and team performance: an empirical study", Journal of Management", Vol. 18, No 8, pp 694-705

Rico, R., Sanchez-Manzanares, M., Gil, F., Gibson, C., 2008, "Team Implicit Coordination Processes: A Team Knowledge-Based Approach", Academy of management Review, Vol. 33, No 1, pp 163-184

Rosnet, E., Jurion, S., Cazes, G., Bachelard, C., 2004, "Mixed-gender groups: coping strategies and factors of psychological adaptation in a polar environment", Aviation, Space and Environmental Medicine, Vol. 75 No. 7, Section 2.

Sargent, L.D., Sue-Chan, C., 2001, "Does Diversity Affect Group Efficacy? The Intervening Role of Cohesion and Task Interdependence", Small Group Research, Vol. 32, No 4, pp 426-450

Satpathy, J., 2012, "Issues in Neuro-Management Decision making", Opinion: International Journal of Business management, Vol. 2, No 2, pp 23-36

Schermerhorn, J. R., Hunt, J. G., Osborn, R. N., 2003, Organizational Behavior, Wiley, New York

Schmidt, L.L., Wood, J., Lugg, D.J., 2004, "Tem Climate at Antarctic Research Stations 1996-2000: Leadership Matters", Aviation, Space, and Environmental Medicine, Vol. 75, No 8, pp. 681-687

Senior, B., 1997, "Team Performance: using repertory grid technique to gain a view from the inside", Team Performance Management, Vol. 3, No 1, pp 33-39

Steel, G.D., 2005, "Whole Lot of Parts: Stress in Extreme Environments", Aviation, Space, and Environmental Medicine, Vol. 76, No 6, pp. 67-73

Stewart, C-B., 1993, "The powers and pitfalls of parsimony", Nature, Vol. 361, pp. 603-607

Stewart, G.L., 2006, "A Meta-Analytic Review of Relationships Between Team Design Features and Team Performance", Journal of Management, Vol. 32, No 1

Strebel, P., 1996, "Why Do Employees Resist Change?", edit. in Harvard Business Review on Change, USA, pp.139-157

Tarricone, P., Luca, J., 2002, "Employees, teamwork and social interdependence – a formula for successful business?", Team Performance Management: An International Journal, Vol. 8, No 3/4, pp 54-59

Tracey, T.J.G., Ryan, J.M., Jaschik-Herman, B., 2001, "Complementarity of Interpersonal Circumplex Traits", Personality and Social Psychology Bulletin, Vol. 27, No 7, pp 786-797

West, M. A., 2004, Effective Teamwork: practical lessons from organizational research, 2nd edition, BPS Blackwell, UK

Bibliography

I write best when I am writing freely, without contextualizing my thoughts. However, all proposed theories and models would have never been realized without the previous work of other authors and researchers. My own perspective of management and leadership surfaced in my mind after studying their theories and studies. Hereunder, in addition to the references, you may find the main sources of my knowledge tank for creating the current book.

Abbott, J.B., Boyd, N.G., Miles, G., 2006, "Does type of team matter? An investigation of the relationships between job characteristics and outcomes within a team-based environment", The Journal of Social Psychology, Vol. 146, No 4, pp 485-507

Adams, R.S., Tracey, T.J.G., 2004, "Three Versions of the Interpersonal Adjective Scales and Their Fit to the Circumplex Model", Assessment, Vol. 11, No 3, pp 263-270

Allen, N.J., Hecht, T.D., 2004, "The 'romance of teams': Toward an understanding of its psychological underpinnings and implications", Journal of Occupational and Organizational Psychology, Vol. 77, pp 439-461

Arthur, W. Jr, Woehr, D.J., Graziano, W.G., 2001, "Personality testing in employment settings. Problems and issues in the application of typical selection practices", Personnel Review, Vol. 30, No 6, pp 657-676

Ashton, M.C., 1998, "Personality and job performance: the importance of narrow traits", Journal of Organizational Behavior, Vol. 19, pp 289-303

Ashton, M.C., Lee, K., 2001, "A Theoretical Basis for the Major Dimensions of Personality", European Journal of Personality, Vol. 15, pp 327-353

Balderson, S.J., Broderick, A.J., 1996, "Behaviour in teams: exploring occupational and gender differences", Journal of Managerial Psychology, Vol. 11, No 5, pp 33-42

Barrick, M.R., Mount, M.K., 1993, "Autonomy as a Moderator of the Relationships Between the Big Five Personality Dimensions and Performance", Journal of Applied Psychology, Vol. 78, No 1, pp 111-118

Bauer, J., 2008, Learning from Errors at Work: Studies on Nurses' Engagement in Error-Related Learning Activities, PhD Thesis, University of Regensburg, Regensburg

Belbin, R.M., 1981, 1988, Management Teams. Why They Succeed or Fail. Butterworth-Heinemann Ltd, Oxford

Biersner, R.J., Hogan, R., 1984, "Personality Correlates of Adjustment in Isolated Work Groups", Journal of Research in Personality, Vol. 18, pp. 491-496

Bishop, J.W., Scott, K.D., Burroughs, S.M., 2000, "Support, Commitment, and Employee Outcomes in a Team Environment", Journal of Management, Vol. 26, No 6, pp 1113-1132

Blackman, M.C., 2002, "Personality Judgment and the Utility of the Unstructured Employment Interview", Basic and Applied Social Psychology, Vol. 24, No 3, pp 241-250

Borman, W.C., Motowidlo, S.J., 1997, "Task Performance and Contextual Performance: The Meaning for Personnel Selection Research", Human Performance, Vol. 10, No 2, pp 99-109

Bradley, J.H., Hebert, F.J., 1997, "The effect of personality type on team performance", Journal of Management Development, Vol. 16, No 5, pp 337-353

Campion, M.A., Medsker, G.H., Higgs, C.A., 1993, "Relations between work group characteristics and effectiveness: Implications for designing effective work groups", Personnel Psychology, Vol. 46, pp 823-850

Carlo, G., Okun, M.A., Knight, G.P., de Guzman, M.R.T., 2005, "The interplay of traits and motives on volunteering: agreeableness, extraversion and prosocial valued motivation", Personality and Individual Differences, Vol. 38, pp 1293-1305

Clark, R.E., 2005, "5 Research-Tested Team Motivation Strategies", Performance Improvement", Vol. 44, No 1, pp 13-16

Costa, P.T., Jr., McCrae, R.R., 1995, "Primary Traits of Eysenck's P-E-N System: Three- and Five-Factor Solutions", Journal of Personality and Social Psychology, Vol. 69, No 2, pp 308-317

Davies, M.F., Kanaki, E., 2006, "Interpersonal characteristics associated with different team roles in work groups", Journal of Managerial Psychology, Vol. 21, No 7, pp 638-650

Day, A.L., Carroll, S.A., 2004, "Using an ability-based measure of emotional intelligence to predict individual performance, group performance, and group citizenship behaviours", Personality and Individual Differences, Vol. 36, pp 1443-1458

De Cremer, D., 2002, "Respect and Cooperation in Social Dilemmas: The Importance of Feeling Included", Personality and Social Psychology Bulletin, Vol. 28, No 10, pp 1335-1341

De Raad, B., 2005, "The trait-coverage of emotional intelligence", Personality and Individual Differences, Vol. 38, pp 673-687

Devine, D.J., 2002, "A Review and Integration of Classification Systems Relevant to Teams in Organizations", Group Dynamics: Theory, and Practice, Vol. 6, No 4, pp 291-310

Devine, D.J., Philips, J.L., 2001, "Do Smarter Teams Do Better? A Meta-Analysis of Cognitive Ability and Team Performance", Small Group Research, Vol. 32, No, 5, pp 507-532

Digman, J.M., 1990, "Personality Structure: Emergence of the five factor model", Annual Review of Psychology, Vol. 41, pp 417-440

Driskell, J.E., Salas, E., 1991, "Group Decision Making Under Stress", Journal of Applied Psychology, Vol. 76, No 3, pp 473-478

Eby, L.T., Dobbins, G.H., 1997, "Collectivistic orientation in teams: an individual and group-level analysis", Journal of Organizational Behavior, Vol. 18, pp 275-295

Eckel, C. C., Grossman, P. J., 2005, "Managing Diversity by Creating Team Identity", Journal of Economic Behaviour and Organization, Vol. 58, pp 371-392

English, A., Griffith, R.L., Steelman, L.A., 2004, "Team Performance: The Effect of Team Conscientiousness and Task Type", Small Group Research, Vol. 35, No 6, pp 643-665

Fay, D., Frese, M., 2001, "The Concept of Personal Initiative: An Overview of Validity Studies", Human Performance, Vol. 14, No 1, pp 97-124

Finkel, E.J., Campbell, W.K., Brunell, A.B, Dalton, A.N., Scarbeck, S.J., Chartrand, T.L., 2006, "High-Maintenance Interaction: Inefficient Social Coordination Impairs Self-Regulation", Journal of Personality and social Psychology, Vol. 91, No 3, pp 456-475

Fisher, S.G., Hunter, T.A., Macrosson, W.D.K., 2002, "Belbin's team role theory: for non-managers also?", Journal of Managerial Psychology, Vol. 17, No 1, pp 14-20

Fisher, S.G., Macrosson, W.D.K., Wong, J, 1998, "Cognitive style and team role preference", Journal of Managerial Psychology, Vol. 13, No 8, pp 544-557

Fletcher, C., Bailey, C., 2003, "Assessing self-awareness: some issues and methods", Journal of Managerial Psychology, Vol. 18, No 5, pp 395-404

Fletcher, C., Baldry, C., 2000, "A study of individual differences and self-awareness in the context of multi-source feedback", Journal of Occupational and Organizational Psychology, Vol. 73, pp 303-319

Flin, R.H., 1997, "Crew resource management for teams in the offshore oil industry", Team Performance Management, Vol. 3, No 2, pp 121-129

Forsyth, D. R., (1999), Group Dynamics, 3rd edition, Wadsworth, USA

Foushee, H.C., 1984, "Dyads and Triads at 35,000 Feet: Factors Affecting Group Process and Aircrew Performance", American Psychologist, Vol. 39, No 8, pp 885-893

Frese, M., Fay, D., Hilburger, T., Leng, K., Tag, A., 1997, "The concept of personal initiative: Operationalization, reliability and validity in two German samples", Journal of Occupational and Organizational Psychology, Vol. 70, pp 139-161

Gladstein, D.L., 1984, "Groups in Context: A Model of Task Group Effectiveness", Administrative Science Quarterly, Vol. 29, pp 499-517

Gottfredson, G.D., Jones, E.M., Holland, J.L., 1993, "Personality and Vocational Interests: The Relations of Holland's Six Interest Dimensions to Five Robust Dimensions of Personality", Journal of Counselling Psychology, Vol. 40, No 4, pp. 518-524

Gruenfeld, D.H., Mannix, E.A., Williams, K.Y., Neale, M.A., 1996, "Group Composition and Decision Making: How Member Familiarity and Information Distribution Affect Process and Performance", Organizational Behavior and Human Decision Processes, Vol. 67, No 1, pp 1-15

Gundlach, M., Zivnuska, S., Stoner, J., 2006, "Understanding the relationship between individualism-collectivism and team performance through an integration of social identity theory and the social relations model", Human Relations, Vol. 59, No 12, pp 1603-1632

Halfhill, T, Nielsen, T.M., Sundstrom, E., Weilbaecher, A., 2005, "Group Personality Composition and Performance in Military Service Teams", Military Psychology, Vol. 17, No 1, pp 41-54

Hayes, N., 1997, Successful Team Management, ITP, U.K

Hollenbeck, J.R., DeRue, D.S., Guzzo, R., 2004, "Bridging the Gap Between I/O Research and HR Practice: Improving Team Composition, Team Training, and Team Task Design", Human Resource Management, Vol. 43, No 4, pp 353-366

Hough, L.M. & Oswald, F.L., 2000, "Personnel Selection: Looking Toward the Future – Remembering the Past", Annual Review of Psychology, Vol. 51, pp 631-664

Hough, L.M., 1992, "The "Big Five" Personality Variables – Construct Confusion: Description Versus Prediction", Human Performance, Vol. 5, No 1&2, pp 139-155

Housel, D. J., 2002, Team Dynamics, South-Western, USA

Immordino-Yang, M.H., Christodoulou, J.A., Singh, V., 2012, "Rest Is Not Idleness: Implications of the Brain's Default Mode for Human Development and Education", *Perspectives on Psychological Science*, Vol. 7, No 4, pp. 352-364

Ingram, H., Desombre, T., 1999, "Teamwork: comparing academic and practitioners' perceptions", Team Performance Management, Vol. 5, No 1, pp 16-22

Ivkovic, V., Vitart, V., Rudan., I., et al., 2007, "The Eysenck personality factors: Psychometric structure, reliability, heritability and phenotypic and genetic correlations with psychological distress in an isolated Croatian population", Personality and Individual Differences, Vol. 42, pp 123-133

Jehn, A.K., Northcraft, B.G., Neale, A.M., 1999, "Why Differences Make a Difference: A Field Study of Diversity, Conflict, and Performance in Workgroups", Administrative Science Quarterly, Vol. 44, pp 741-763

John, O.P., Srivastava, S., 1999, The Big-Five Taxonomy: History, Measurement, and Theoretical Perspectives, [on line], University of California at Berkeley. Available from: www.uoregon.edu/~sanjay/pubs/bigfive.pdf

Jones, P.E., Roelofsma, P.H.M.P., 2000, "The potential for social contextual and group biases in team decision-making: biases, conditions and psychological mechanisms", Ergonomics, Vol. 43, No 8, pp 1129-1152

Judge, T.A., Jackson, C.L., Shaw, J.C., Scott, B.A., Rich, B.L., 2007, "Self-Efficacy and Work-Related Performance: The Integral Role of Individual Differences", Journal of Applied Psychology, Vol. 92, No 1, pp 107-127

Kanfer, R., Ackerman, P.L., 2000, "Individual Differences in Work Motivation: Further Explorations of a Trait Framework", Applied Psychology: An International Review, Vol. 49, No 3, pp 470-482

Keinan, G., 1987, "Decision Making Under Stress: Scanning of Alternatives Under Controllable and Uncontrollable Threats", Journal of Personality and Social Psychology, Vol. 52, No 3, pp 639-644

Kensinger, E.A., 2007, "Negative Emotion Enhances Memory Accuracy: Behavioral and Neuroimaging Evidence", Association for Psychological Science, Vo. 16, No. 4, pp. 213-218

Kichuk, S.L., Wiesner, W.H., 1997, "The Big Five personality factors and team performance: implications for selecting successful product design teams", Journal of Engineering and Technology Management, Vol. 14, pp 195-221

Kichuk, S.L., Wiesner, W.H., 1998, "Work Teams: Selecting Members for Optimal Performance", Canadian Psychology, Vol. 39, No 1-2, pp 23-32

Kirkman, B.L., Tesluk, P.E., Rosen B., 2004, "The Impact of Demographic Heterogeneity and Team Leader-Team Member Demographic Fit on Team Empowerment and Effectiveness", Group & Organization Management, Vol. 29, No 3, pp 334-368

Larson, L.M., Rottinghaus, P.J., Borgen, F.H., 2002, "Meta-analyses of Big Six Interests and Big Five Personality Factors, Journal of Vocational Behavior, Vol. 61, pp 217-239

Lau, D.C., Murnighan, J.K., 1998, "Demographic Diversity and Faultlines: The Compositional Dynamics of Organizational Groups", Academy of Management Review", Vol. 23, No 2, pp 325-340

LePine, J.A., Hollenbeck, J.R., Ilgen, D.R., Hedlund, J., 1997, "Effects of Individual Differences on the Performance of Hierarchical Decision-Making Teams: Much More Than g" Journal of Applied Psychology, Vol. 82, No 5, pp 803-811

Liao, W-C., Tsai, C-C., 2001, "A study of cockpit crew teamwork behaviours", Team Performance Management, Vol. 7, No 1/ 2, pp 21-26

Locke, K.D., Sadler, P, 2007, "Self-Efficacy, Values, and Complementarity in Dyadic Interactions: Integrating Interpersonal and Social-Cognitive Theory", Personality and Social Psychology Bulletin, Vol. 33, No 1, pp 94-109

Malone, T.W., Crowston, K., 1993, "The Interdisciplinary Study of coordination", ACM Computing Surveys, Vol. 26, No 1, pp 87-119

Matthews, G, Emo, A.K., Funke, G., Zeidner, M., Roberts, R.D., Costa, P.T.Jr, Schulze, R., 2006, "Emotional Intelligence, Personality, and Task-Induced Stress", Journal of Experimental Psychology, Vol. 12, No 2, pp 96-107

McClough, A.C., Rogelberg, S.G., 2003, "Selection in Teams: An Exploration of the Teamwork Knowledge, Skills, and Ability Test", International Journal of Selection and Assessment, Vol. 11, No 1, pp 56-66

McElroy, T., Dowd, K., 2007, "Susceptibility to anchoring effects: How openness-to-experience influences responses to anchoring cues", *Judgment and Decision Making*, Vol. 2, No. 1, pp. 48-53

McGrath, J.E., Arrow, H., Berdahl, J.L., 2000, "The Study of Groups: Past, Present, and Future", Personality and Social Psychology Review, Vol. 4, No 1, pp 95-105

Miller, D.L., 2001, "Reexamining Teamwork KSAs and Team Performance", Small Group Research, Vol. 32, No 6, pp 745-766

Mohammed, S., 2001, "Toward an Understanding of Cognitive Consensus in a Group Decision-Making Context", *The Journal of Applied Behavioral Science*, Vol. 37, No 4, pp 408-425

Molleman, E., 2005, "Diversity in Demographic Characteristics, Abilities and Personality Traits: Do Faultlines Affect Team Functioning?, Group Decision and Negotiation, Vol. 14, pp 173-193

Morgeson, F.P., Reider, M.H., Campion, M.A., 2005, "Selecting Individuals in Team Settings: The Importance of Social Skills, Personality Characteristics, and Teamwork Knowledge", Personnel Psychology, Vol. 58, pp 583-611

Motowidlo, S.J., Borman, W.C., Schmit, M.J., 1997, "A Theory of Individual Differences in Task and Contextual Performance", Human Performance, Vol. 10, No 2, pp 71-83

Mount, M.K., Barrick, M.R., Strauss, J.P., 1999, "The Joint Relationship of Conscientiousness and Ability with Performance: Test of the Interaction Hypothesis", Journal of Management, Vol. 25, No 5, pp 707-721

O'Connor, M., 2006, "A review of factors affecting individual performance in team environments: Theories and implications for library management", Library Management, Vol. 27, No 3, pp 135-143

Oppezzo, M., Schwartz, D.L., 2014, "Give Your Ideas Some Legs: The Positive Effect of Walking on Creative Thinking", *Jouran of Experimental Psychology: learning, Memory, and Cognition*, online http://dx.doi.org/10.1037/a0036577

Peeters, M.A.G., Van Tuijl, H.F.J.M., Rutte, C.G., Reymen, I.M.M.J., 2006, "Personality and Team Performance: A Meta-Analysis", European Journal of Personality, Vol. 20, pp 377-396

Pelled, L.H., 1996, "Demographic Diversity, Conflict, and Work Group Outcomes: An Intervening Process Theory", Organization Science, Vol. 7, No 6, pp 615-631

Petrides, K.V., Furnham, A., 2001, "Trait Emotional Intelligence: Psychometric Investigation with Reference to Established Trait Taxonomies", European Journal of Personality, Vol. 15, pp 425-448

Porter, C.O.L.H., Hollenbeck, J.R., Ilgen, D.R., Ellis, A.P.J., West, B.J., Moon, H., 2003, "Backing Up Behaviors in Teams: The Role of Personality and Legitimacy of Need", Journal of Applied Psychology, Vol. 88, No 3, pp 391-403

Prichard, J.S., Stanton, N.A., 1999, "Testing Belbin's team role theory of effective groups", The journal of Management Development, Vol. 18, No 8, pp 652-665

Pulakos E.D., Performance Management: a roadmap for developing, implementing and evaluating performance management systems, 2004, SHRM Foundation, USA

Rach, S. Ufer, S., Heinze, A., 2013, "Learning from errors: effects of teachers' training on students' attitudes towards and their individual use of errors, PNA, Vol. 8, No. 1, pp. 21-30

Reilly, R.R., Lynn, G.S., Aronson, Z.H., 2002, "The role of personality in new product development team performance", Journal of Engineering and Technology Management, Vol. 19, pp 39-58

Rico, R., Molleman, E., Sanchez-Manzanares, M., Van der Vegt, G., 2007, "The Effects of Diversity Faultlines and Team Task Autonomy on Decision Quality and Social Integration", Journal of Management, Vol. 33, No 1, pp 111-132

Rothblum, E.K., 1990, "Psychological Factors in the Antarctic", The Journal of Psychology, Vol. 124, No 3, pp 253-273

Rushmer, R.K., 1996, "Is Belbin's shaper really TMS's thrusters-organizer? An empirical investigation into the correspondence between the Belbin and TMS team role models", Leadership & Organization Development Journal, Vol. 17, No 1, pp 20-26

Salas E., Rozell, D, Mullen, B., Driskell, J.E., 1999, "The Effect of Team Building on Performance: An Integration", Small Group Research, Vol. 30, No 3, pp 309-329

Salovey, P., Grewal, D., 2005, "The Science of Emotional Intelligence", Current Directions in Psychological Science, Vol. 14, No 6, pp 281-285

Sarris, A., 2007, "Antarctic Culture: 50 Years of Antarctic Expeditions", Aviation, Space, and Environmental Medicine, Vol. 78, No 9, pp. 886-892

Schaubroeck, J., Lam, S.S.K., Cha, S.E., 2007, "Embracing Transformational Leadership: Team Values and the Impact of Leader Behavior on Team Performance", Journal of Applied Psychology, Vol. 92, No 4, pp 1020-1030

Schwartz, S.J., Waterman, A.S., 2006, "Changing interests: A longitudinal study of intrinsic motivation for personally salient activities", Journal of Research in Personality, Vol. 40, pp 1119-1136

Shamir, B, 1990, "Calculations, Values, and Identities: The Sources of Collectivistic Work Motivation", Human Relations, Vol. 43, No 4, pp 313-332

Shapcott, K.M., Carron, A.V., Burke, S.M., Bradshaw, M.H., Estabrooks, P.A., 2006, "Member Diversity and Cohesion and Performance in Walking Groups", Small Group Research, Vol. 37, No 6, pp 701-720

Sommerville, J., Dalziel, S., 1998, "Project teambuilding-the applicability of Belbin's team-role self-perception inventory", International Journal of Project Management, Vol. 16, No 3, pp 165-171

Stanton, N., Matthews, G., 1995, "Twenty-one traits of personality: An alternative solution for the occupational personality questionnaire", Journal of Management Development, Vol. 14, No 7, pp 66-75

Stevens, M.J., Campion, M.A., 1999, "Staffing Work Teams: Development and Validation of a Selection Test for Teamwork Settings", Journal of Management, Vol. 25, No 2, pp 207-228

Stewart, G.L., Barrick, M.R., 2000, "Team Structure and Performance: Assessing the Mediating Role of Intrateam Process and the Moderating Role of Task Type", Academy of Management Journal, Vol. 43, No 2, pp 135-148

Stewart, G.L., Fulmer, I.S., Barrick, M.R., 2005, "An Exploration of Member Roles as a Multilevel Linking Mechanism for Individual Traits and Team Outcomes", Personnel Psychology, Vol. 58, pp 343-365

Stout, J.R., Salas, E., Carson, R., 1994, "Individual Task Proficiency and Team Process Behavior: What's Important for Team Functioning?", Military Psychology", Vol. 6, No 3, pp 177-192

Sue-Chan, C., Latham, G.P., 2004, "The Situational Interview as a Predictor of Academic and Team Performance: A Study of the Mediating Effects of Cognitive Ability and Emotional Intelligence", International Journal of Selection and Assessment, Vol. 12, No 4, pp 321-320

Sundstrom, E., Busby, P.L., Bobrow, W.S., 1997, "Group Process and Performance: Interpersonal Behaviors and Decision Quality in Group Problem Solving by Consensus", Group Dynamics: Theory, Research and Practice, Vol. 1, No 3, pp 241-253

Sundstrom, E., McIntyre, M., Halfhill, T., Richards, H., 2000, "Work Groups: From the Hawthorne Studies to Work Teams of the 1990s and Beyond", Group Dynamics: Theory, Research, and Practice, Vol. 4, No 1, pp 44-67

Tjosvold, D., Field, R.H.G., 1985, "Effect of Concurrence, Controversy, and Consensus on Group Decision Making", The Journal of Social Psychology, Vol. 125, No 3, pp 355-363

Tracey, T.J.G., 2004, "Levels of Interpersonal Complementarity: A Simplex Representation", Personality and Social Psychology Bulletin, Vol. 30, No 9, pp 1211-1225

Tyler, R.T., Blader, S.L., 2001, "Identity and cooperative behavior in groups", Group Processes & Intergroup Relations, Vol. 4, No 3, pp 207-226

Van Der Zee, K., Thijs, M., Schakel, L., 2002, "The Relationship of Emotional Intelligence with Academic Intelligence and the Big Five", European Journal of Personality, Vol. 16, pp 103-125

Volkema, R.J., Gorman, R.H., 1998, "The Influence of Cognitive-Based Group Composition on Decision-Making Process and Outcome", Journal of Management Studies, Vol. 35, No 1, pp 105-121

Webber, S.S., Donahue, L.M., 2001, "Impact of highly and less job-related diversity on work group cohesion and performance: a meta-analysis", Journal of Management, Vol. 27, pp 141-162

Wiggins, J.S., Trapnell, P., Phillips, N., 1988, "Psychometric and Geometric Characteristics of the Revised Interpersonal Adjective Scales (IAS-R)", Multivariate Behavioral Research, Vol. 23, pp 517-530

Witt, L.A., 2002, "The Interactive Effects of Extraversion and Conscientiousness on Performance", Journal of Management, Vol. 28, No 6, pp 835-851

Witt, L.A., Burke, L.A., Barrick, M.R., Mount, M.K., 2002b, "The Interactive Effects of Conscientiousness and Agreeableness on Job Performance", Journal of Applied Psychology, Vol. 87, No 1, pp 164-169

Witt, L.A., Hilton, T.F., Hochwarter, W.A., 2001, "Addressing Politics in Matrix Teams", Group & Organization Management, Vol. 26, No 2, pp 230-247

Witt, L.A., Kacmar, K.M., Carlson, D.S., Zivnuska, S., 2002, "Interactive effects of personality and organizational politics on contextual performance", Journal of Organizational Behavior, Vol. 23, pp 911-926

Young, M., Dulewicz, V., 2007, "Relationships between emotional and congruent self-awareness and performance in the British Royal Navy", Journal of Managerial Psychology, Vol. 22, No 5, pp. 465-478

Zeidner, M., Matthews, G., Roberts, R.D., 2004, "Emotional Intelligence in the Workplace: A Critical Review", Applied Psychology: An International Review, Vol. 53, No 3, pp 371-399

www.ingramcontent.com/pod-product-compliance
Lightning Source LLC
Chambersburg PA
CBHW022037190326
41520CB00008B/620